ACCLAIM FOR Peter Mayle

"Engaging. . . . Enthusiastic paeans to olive oil, truffles, and bouillabaisse, washed down with a good local
vintage or a glass of pastis."
    —Michael Dirda, *The Washington Post Book World*

"The glories of the French countryside come alive."
                              —*The Hartford Courant*

"Stylish, witty, delightfully readable."
                              —*The Sunday Times* (London)

"[Mayle] virtually establishes a lip-licking new literary
genre—call it dinnerotica. . . . He is becoming an
American Evelyn Waugh."   —*People*

"As charming and witty as ever. . . . Mayle enticingly re-
counts his peregrinations around the truffle markets
and his searches for the perfect corkscrew or melon,
but it's his ability to capture the subtle cultural pecu-
liarities that distinguishes his writing."
                              —*Publishers Weekly*

"[Mayle has] a journalist's eye for detail and a novelist's
sense of character."   —*San Francisco Chronicle*

Peter Mayle

Encore Provence

Peter Mayle spent fifteen years in the advertising business, first as a copywriter and then as a reluctant executive, before escaping Madison Avenue to write books. He is the author of *A Year in Provence* and *Toujours Provence*, as well as the novels *Hotel Pastis, A Dog's Life, Anything Considered,* and *Chasing Cézanne*.

Encore Provence

Encore Provence

New Adventures in the

South of France

Peter Mayle

VINTAGE DEPARTURES
Vintage Books
A Division of Random House, Inc.
New York

FIRST VINTAGE DEPARTURES EDITION, MAY 2000

The Library of Congress has cataloged the Knopf edition as follows:
Mayle, Peter
Encore Provence : new adventures in the south of France / Peter Mayle.
p. cm.
ISBN 0-679-44124-7
1. Mayle, Peter—Homes and haunts—France—Provence.
2. Provence (France)—Social life and customs. I. Title.
DC611.P961 M34 1999b
944'.9—dc21 99-62335
CIP

Vintage ISBN: 0-679-76269-8

Author photograph © Jennie Mayle

www.vintagebooks.com

Printed in the United States of America
10 9 8 7 6 5 4 3 2 1

For Jennie with love, *comme toujours*

Contents

Encore Provence

Second Impressions

I think it was the sight of a man power-washing his underpants that really brought home the differences, cultural and otherwise, between the old world and the new.

It was a cold, still morning in early winter, and the pulsing *thumpthump, thumpthump* of a high-pressure hose echoed through the village. Getting closer to the sound, it was possible to see, over a garden wall, a laundry line totally devoted to gentlemen's underwear in a stimulating assortment of colors. The garments were under attack, jerking and flapping under the force of the water jet like hanging targets in a shooting gallery. Standing some distance away, out of ricochet range, was the aggressor, in cap and muffler and ankle-high zippered carpet slippers. He had adopted the classic stance of a soldier in combat, feet spread apart, shooting from the hip, a merciless hail of droplets raking back and forth. The underpants didn't stand a chance.

Only a few days before, my wife and I and the dogs had arrived back in Provence after an absence of four years. Much of that time had been spent in America, where we were able to slip back into the comfortable familiarity of a language that was relatively free—although not entirely—from the problems of being socially appropriate or sexually accurate. No longer did we have to ponder the niceties of addressing people as *vous* or *tu,* or to rush to the dictionary to check on the gender of everything from a peach to an aspirin. English was spoken, even if our ears were rusty and some of the fashionable linguistic flourishes took a little getting used to.

A friend of below-average height told us he was not considered short any more but "vertically challenged"; the hour, previously a plain old sixty minutes, had sprouted a "top" and a "bottom"; you were not seen leaving a room, but "exiting" it; the economy was regularly being "impacted," as though it were a rogue wisdom tooth; great minds "intuited" where once they had merely guessed; "hopefully," an agreeable word that never harmed a soul, was persistently abused. Important people didn't change their opinions, but underwent a significant "tactical recalibration."

There were many and hideous outbreaks of legalese in everyday speech, reflecting the rise of litigation as a national spectator sport. "Surplusage" was one of a hundred of these horrors. I noticed also that sophisticated and influential Americans—those whose comments are sought by the media—were not content to finish anything but preferred to "reach closure," and I have a nasty feeling that it won't be long before this affectation is picked up by waiters in pretentious restaurants. I can hear it already: "Have you reached closure on your salad?" (This, of course, would only be after you had spent some time bending your "learning curve" around the menu.)

We met, for the first time, the "outster," although we never saw a trace of his more fortunate relative, the inster. We were taught to give up our hopelessly old-fashioned habit of concentrating and instead try "focusing." Every day seemed to bring new and exciting vocabulary options. But these minor curiosities didn't alter the fact that we were surrounded by at least some version of the mother tongue and therefore should have felt quite at home.

Somehow we didn't, although it certainly wasn't for lack of a welcome. Almost everyone we met lived up to the American reputation for friendliness and generosity. We had settled in a house outside East Hampton, on the far end of Long Island, a part of the world that, for nine months a year, is quiet and extremely beautiful. We wallowed in the convenience of America, in the efficiency and the extraordinary variety of choice, and we practiced native customs. We came to know California wines. We shopped by phone. We drove sedately. We took vitamins and occasionally remembered to worry about cholesterol. We tried to watch television. I gave up taking cigars to restaurants, but smoked them furtively in private. There was even a period when we drank eight glasses of water a day. In other words, we did our best to adapt.

And yet there was something missing. Or rather, an entire spectrum of sights and sounds and smells and sensations that we had taken for granted in Provence, from the smell of thyme in the fields to the swirl and jostle of Sunday-morning markets. Very few weeks went by without a twinge of what I can best describe as homesickness.

Returning to a place where you have been happy is generally regarded as a mistake. Memory is a notoriously biased and sentimental editor, selecting what it wants to keep and invariably making a few cosmetic changes to past events. With rose-colored hindsight, the good times become magical; the bad times fade and eventually disappear, leaving only a seductive blur of sunlit days and the laughter of friends. Was it really like that? Would it be like that again?

There was, of course, only one way to find out.

For everyone coming to France directly from America, the first and most nerve-wracking shock to the system is traffic shock, and it hit us as soon as we left the airport. Instantly, we were sucked into high-velocity chaos, menaced on all sides by a hurtle of small cars driven, it seemed, by bank robbers making a getaway. The Frenchman on wheels, as we were quickly reminded, sees every car in front of him as a challenge, to be overtaken on either side, on blind bends, while lights are changing or when road signs are advising prudence. The highway speed limit of eighty miles an hour is considered to be an insufferable restriction of personal liberty, or perhaps some quaint regulation for tourists, and is widely ignored.

It wouldn't be so alarming if the equipment, both human and mechanical, were up to the demands placed on it. But you can't help feeling, as yet another baby Renault screams past with its tires barely touching the road, that small cars were never designed to break the sound barrier. Nor are you filled with confidence if you should catch a glimpse of what's going on behind the wheel. It is well known that the Frenchman cannot put two sentences together without his hands joining in. Fingers must wag in emphasis. Arms must be thrown up in dismay. The orchestra of speech must be conducted. This performance may be entertaining when you watch a couple of men arguing in a bar, but it's heart-stopping when you see it in action at ninety miles an hour.

And so it's always a relief to get onto the back roads where you can travel at the speed of a tractor, with time to take in some of the graphic additions to the scenery. Ever since my first visit to Provence I have loved the faded advertisements painted on the sides of barns and solitary stone *cabanons*—invitations to try aperitifs that have long since vanished, or chocolate, or fertilizer—the paint chipped and peeling, the blues and the ochres and the creams bleached by the sun of seventy or eighty summers.

For years, these primitive billboards have been outnumbered by less picturesque messages, and these seem to be increasing. Towns and villages now often have two names, one with the old Provençal spelling. So Ménerbes now doubles as Menerbo, Avignon as Avignoun, Aix as Aix-en-Prouvenço. And this may only be the start. If the Provençal road-sign lobby continues to be active, we might one day see *Frequent Radar Controls* or *Low-Flying Aircraft* or even *The Home of the Big Mac* adapted to the language of Frédéric Mistral's poetry.

Signs are everywhere—informative, persuasive, educational, proprietorial, nailed on trees, perched on poles by the side of a field, attached to railings, pasted onto concrete; signs for wine *caves,* for honey, for lavender essence and olive oil, for restaurants and real estate agents. Most are inviting. But there are a few which warn of savage dogs, and one—my favorite—is particularly discouraging. I saw it in the hills of Haute Provence, tied to the trunk of a tree by the side of a path leading into a stretch of seem-

ingly uninhabited wilderness. It read as follows: *Tout con-
trevenant sera abattu, les survivants poursuivis.* Which,
roughly translated, means: *Trespassers will be shot. Survivors will be prosecuted.* I like to believe that the author
had a sense of humor.

There is one other warning I can't imagine seeing anywhere else in the world but France. You can find it in the
Place des Lices, in St.-Tropez, where the market is held
every week, an enamel sign screwed to the railings. It
informs the passer-by in large type and stern language that
he is absolutely forbidden to stop and relieve himself in
the vicinity—a message one cannot imagine being necessary in East Hampton, for instance, a town noted for its
well-toned and highly disciplined bladders.

The message is necessary in France because of the
Frenchman's fondness for impromptu urination. Whenever nature calls, he is quick to answer, and it doesn't matter where he finds himself at the time. In towns and cities
there are a thousand discreet corners; out here in the
country, hundreds of empty square miles and millions of
bushes ensure privacy for *le pipi rustique.* But judging by
what I've seen of the Frenchman's choice of venue, privacy is the last thing that he wants. Sometimes on a rock,
silhouetted against the sky like a stag at bay, sometimes so
close to the side of the road that you have to swerve to
avoid cutting him off in midstream, he is there, doing
what a man has to do. And he has not the slightest embar-
rassment about doing it. If you should catch his eye as you
pass, he will acknowledge you with a courteous nod. But it
is more likely that he will be gazing upward, counting the
clouds as he takes his ease.

Luckily, such forbidding notices are not at all typical of
the greeting one can expect in most public places. The

politeness of strangers in France is noticeable—not necessarily friendly but invariably well-mannered, and a morning of running errands is marked at every stop by small but pleasant acknowledgments that you exist, something that doesn't always happen in other countries. In England, for example, many shopkeepers make a point of behaving as if you're not there, possibly because you haven't been formally introduced. In America, the land of rampant informality, you can frequently find the other extreme, and the customer has to respond to well-meaning inquiries about his overall health and how he's doing followed, if they're not quickly nipped in the bud, by a stream of comments and questions about ancestry, clothing, oddities of pronunciation, and general appearance. The French, it seems to me, strike a happy balance between intimacy and reserve.

Some of this must be helped by the language, which lends itself to graceful expression even when dealing with fairly basic subjects. No, Monsieur, you haven't made a beast of yourself at the table; you're simply suffering from a *crise de foie*. And could that be flatulence we hear coming from the gentleman in the corner? Certainly not. It is the plangent sound of the *piano des pauvres,* the poor man's piano. As for that stomach we see threatening to burst the buttons on your shirt, well, that's nothing but a *bonne brioche*. And there is that famously elegant subtitle from a classic Western.

COWBOY: "Gimme a shot of red-eye."
SUBTITLE: *"Un Dubonnet, s'il vous plaît."*

No wonder French was the language of diplomacy for all those years.

It is still the language of gastronomy, and in a country that often gives the impression—at least on the roads—of being late for lunch or dinner, you would expect to see more physical evidence of the national passion for good food. More solid flesh, more Michelin men rolling from one meal to the next. But it isn't so; not, at least, in Provence. Of course they exist, these mammoths of the table, but they are few. The vast majority of men and women I see every day are definitely, irritatingly slimmer than they have any right to be. I've heard people from other countries explain this as the result of some benign cocktail of the genes, or an overactive metabolism brought on by too much coffee and French politics, but the true answer must lie in what they eat and drink and how they eat and drink it.

The French don't snack. They will tear off the end of a fresh baguette (which, if it's warm, is practically impossible to resist) and eat it as they leave the *boulangerie*. And that's usually all you will see being consumed on the street. Compare that with the public eating and drinking that goes on in America: pizza, hot dogs, nachos, tacos, heroes, potato chips, sandwiches, huge containers of coffee, half-gallon buckets of Coke (Diet, of course), and heaven knows what else being demolished on the hoof, often on the way to the aerobics class.

Restraint between meals is rewarded as soon as a Frenchman sits down at the table, and this is where other nationalities become deeply puzzled. How is it possible for a body to pack in two serious meals a day without turning into a human balloon or keeling over with arteries that are rigid with cholesterol? French portions are fairly modest, certainly, but they never stop coming, and they will often include dishes that would horrify doctors in the States:

creamy rillettes of pork, pâtés laced with Armagnac, mushrooms wrapped in buttery pastry, potatoes cooked in duck fat—and these are merely to set you up for the main course. Which, naturally, has to be followed by cheese; but not too much, because dessert is still to come.

And who could contemplate a meal without a glass or two of wine for the stomach's sake? Some years ago, seekers after the gastronomic truth discovered what the French have known for centuries, and pronounced that a little red wine was good for you. Some of them went further. Looking for a tidy explanation of what came to be called the French Paradox, they noticed that the French drink ten times more wine than Americans. *Voilà!* Paradox explained. It must be wine that keeps the French trim and healthy.

I'd like to think it were as simple as that, but I have a feeling that there are other, less dramatic influences at work on and in the French stomach. I believe, without a shred of scientific proof, that the raw ingredients here contain fewer additives, preservatives, colorants, and chemical novelties than in the States. I also believe that food eaten at a table is better for you than food eaten hunched over a desk, standing at a counter, or driving in a car. And I believe that, wherever you do it, hurried eating has ruined more digestive systems than foie gras. Not long ago, there was a fad in certain New York restaurants for the guaranteed thirty-minute lunch, enabling the busy and important executive to entertain two different victims in the space of an hour. If that isn't a recipe for tension and indigestion, I'll swallow my cell phone.

It's true that time in Provence is not worshipped in quite the same way as it is in more hectic parts of the world, and it took me a week or two to bow to the inevitable and put my watch away in a drawer. But while there is no great importance given to time in the sense of punctuality, there is an enormous relish of the moment. Eating, obviously. Conversation on a street corner. A game of *boules*. The choosing of a bunch of flowers. Sitting in a café. Small pleasures receive their due, and there is an absence of rush—sometimes infuriating, often delightful, and in the end contagious. I realized this when I went into town on an errand that need only have taken fifteen minutes, and came back two and a half hours later. I had done absolutely nothing of any importance, and I had enjoyed every minute of it.

Perhaps the slower pace of life is partly responsible for another aspect of the local character, and that is cheerfulness. The French are not famous for being jolly; rather the reverse. Many foreigners tend to judge the mood of the entire nation on the basis of their first humiliating exposure to the Parisian waiter, not knowing that he is as morose and distant toward his countrymen—and probably toward his wife and cat as well—as he is to the tourist. But go south, and the difference is striking. There is an atmosphere of good humor, despite considerable social difficulties, high unemployment, and the financial guillotine of French income tax.

One response to these problems has been to leave them behind, and the newspapers of the moment are filled with stories about young French business people moving from Paris to take advantage of *le boom* in England. But if that kind of ambition exists in Provence, it isn't very apparent. Everyone agrees that times could be better; everyone hopes they will be. Meanwhile, they fall back on the philosophy of the shrug.

It's not a bad philosophy for the visitor to adopt as well, because life in Provence is never short of curiosities, and the national genius for complication is never too far away. There may be some mad logic at work somewhere, but there are many times when it is difficult to understand. Take, for example, the matter of the village garbage dump. It is discreetly placed, frequently cleared, designed to accept debris of any type and size short of a discarded truck, an admirable facility in every way. An official notice is prominently displayed above the garbage containers; translated it reads: *Large items should be deposited two days after the last Wednesday of each month.*

I stood and looked at it one morning for some time, thinking at first that I had misread it, or that my French was letting me down yet again. But no. That's what it said. *Two days after the last Wednesday of each month.* Why didn't it say the last Friday of each month? Was there some plan afoot—doubtless another piece of nonsense from the bureaucrats in Brussels—to change the name of Friday to something more dynamic and politically exciting? Euroday, perhaps. While I was wondering if this was a treat in store for the year 2000, a small van arrived. The driver got out and studied the notice. He looked at me. I looked at him. He looked again at the notice, shook his head and shrugged.

Not long afterward, the notice was removed. I was told that everyone had continued to toss away their old refrigerators, bicycles, and TV sets whenever they felt like it, instructions or no instructions. The French love of signs is only equaled by their delight in ignoring them.

Put this together with another national characteristic, that of keeping your money as much as possible out of the clutches of authority, and you begin to understand the parking problem. Every town in Provence now has areas set aside where you can park your car off the street. These areas, clearly indicated by many signs and thus easy to find, are more often than not ignored. The streets, on the other hand, are clogged with examples of imaginative and illegal parking. Cars with two wheels cocked on the sidewalk or stuffed into alleys with a bare six inches to spare on each side are commonplace. Miracles of stunt driving are performed as traffic backs up, tempers become frayed, horns squawk, and disputes erupt. And why? Because the official parking area has the audacity and the naked greed to charge five francs an hour.

But—so I am assured by my friend Martine, who regularly parks where no others dare to park—it's not just the money. It's the principle. *Le parking payant* is an affront to the French ethos and must be resisted, even if that involves circling the town for half an hour in search of a place. Time, after all, is free. Moral and financial considerations aside, there is also the immense satisfaction to be gained by finding a truly exceptional spot. I once saw a man reverse his small Peugeot into the premises of a boutique that had been gutted prior to renovation. While he was walking away, he looked back at the snug fit of his car in what would one day be a shop window and nodded at it, a moment of bonding between man and machine. It was as if together they had achieved a significant victory.

For me, moments that make up the texture of daily life define the character of Provence as much as the history or the landscape. And if I had to choose a single example of what I missed most in America, it would be a country market; nothing out of the ordinary, just the usual collection of stalls that are set up each week in every town from Apt to Vaison-la-Romaine.

They have an instant visual charm, these markets, with their bursts of vividly colored flowers and vegetables and their handwritten signs, the stalls shaded by ancient plane trees or tucked up against even older stone walls. They might have been artistically arranged for a postcard photographer, or for the high season, to be dismantled and forgotten at the end of summer. But you will find them in January as in August, because their bread and butter come from local inhabitants. The tourist is just a dollop of jam. Welcome, but not essential.

Stall-holders and customers know each other, and so shopping tends to be slow and social. Old Jean-Claude's brand new smile is much admired while he selects some cheese, and there is some debate as to the precisely appropriate texture, given his recently fitted dentures. A Brie would be too sticky. A Mimolette, too hard. Perhaps some Beaufort would be best, until the new teeth have had a chance to settle in. Madame Dalmasso is plunged into a state of profound suspicion by the tomatoes. It is too early in the year for these to be local tomatoes. Where have they come from? Why hasn't their place of birth been written on the sign? After some investigation—a squeeze, a sniff, the lips pursed—she decides to throw caution to the wind and to try half a kilo. A bearded man wanders back to his stall, a glass of rosé in one hand and an infant's feeding bottle in the other. The bottle is for a baby *sanglier* that he has adopted, a tiny wild boar, its black snout twitching at the scent of milk. The flower lady gives my wife her change, then ducks under her stall to reappear with two freshly laid eggs which she gift wraps in a twist of newspaper. On the other side of the square, the tables outside the café are filling up. Above the hiss and clatter of the espresso machine, a voice from Radio Monte Carlo, in raptures of enthusiasm, describes this week's competition. Where do they find these people who never have to stop for breath? Four old men sit in a row on a low stone wall, waiting for the market to end and the square to be cleared so that they can play *boules*. A dog sits up on the wall next to them. All he needs is a flat cap and he'd look just like the men, patient and wrinkled.

As the stall-holders begin to pack up, there is an almost tangible feeling of anticipation. Lunch is in the air, and today it is warm enough to eat outside.

There are two undeserved results of our time on the other side of the Atlantic. The first is that we are thought of as experts in all things American, and are regularly consulted about events taking place in Washington and Hollywood (now almost the same place), as if we knew the politicians and film stars personally. The second is that we are in some way considered responsible for the spread of American tribal customs, and so we often find ourselves pinned to the wall by the accusing finger of Monsieur Farigoule.

A self-appointed guardian of French culture and the purity of the French language, Farigoule can work himself into a lather over everything from *le fast-food* to *les casquettes de baseball*, which have begun to appear on previously bare French heads. But on this particular autumn day, he had something infinitely more grave on his mind, and when he leaped from his bar stool to corner me he was clearly very concerned.

"*C'est un scandale,*" was his opening remark, followed

by a stream of disparaging comments about the pernicious influence of transatlantic imports on the fabric of French rural life. Farigoule is a very small man, almost a miniature, and when agitated tends to bounce up and down on his toes for emphasis, a little ball of outrage. If he were a dog, he'd be a terrier. I asked what had upset him, and found my head going up and down in time with his bouncing.

"*Alowine*," he said. "Is this what we need? The country that gave birth to Voltaire and Racine and Molière, the country that gave Louisiana to the Americans. And what do they give us in return? *Alowine*."

I had no idea what he was talking about, but from his tone of voice and his tightly clamped, downturned mouth it was a major catastrophe, a disaster to rank with a reappearance of phylloxera among the vines or the arrival of Euro Disney outside Paris.

"I don't think I've seen it," I said.

"How could you not? They are everywhere—*les potirons mutilés*—in Apt, in Cavaillon, everywhere."

Mutilated pumpkins could only mean one thing. Like Mickey Mouse and tomato ketchup, Halloween had arrived in France, another nail in the cultural coffin.

After making my excuses, I went into Apt to see for myself. Farigoule had exaggerated, as he usually does, but it was true that Halloween decorations were displayed in one or two shop windows, the first time I had seen them in Provence. I wondered if the population had been officially informed of this addition to the festive calendar, and if they knew what they were supposed to do about it. A random sample interviewed in the streets of Apt revealed only puzzlement. Pumpkins meant soup.

Whose idea had it been to bring Halloween to Provence? And would a health warning be issued to any bands of children allowed out at night to go around the farms on trick-or-treat expeditions? The dogs would get them for sure. Fortunately, the occasion passed without any reports of bloodshed in the local papers. *Alowine,* this year at least, seemed to be one of those parties where nobody showed up.

France, in any case, already has more than enough traditions of its own, which we were rediscovering month by month. There is May, which starts with a public holiday and continues with several more to prepare us for August, when the entire country is *en vacances.* There is a permanent festival of bureaucracy, marked by a snowstorm of paper. Each saint has a saint's day, each village its annual fête. And each week, by popular demand, there is the feast of the common man, otherwise known as Sunday lunch.

Sunday is a day apart, a day that feels different even if one hasn't spent the week in an office. The sounds change. Birdsong and the drone of tractors during the week; the baying of hounds and the pop of distant gunfire on Sunday mornings, when the Provençal hunter likes to exercise his right to defend the countryside from invasion by hostile rabbits and thrushes.

This year, he faces a more serious challenge than ever, from mutant *sangliers.* Nobody seems to know quite how it happened, but the wild boar population has multiplied with dramatic speed. One current theory is that *sangliers*—which normally produce a single small litter each year—have been mating with their more prolific cousin, the domestic pig, and their offspring are threatening to overrun the vineyards and orchards. You can see their calling cards everywhere: ruts gouged out of the earth in the search for food, vegetable gardens trampled, stone walls knocked awry.

The area around our house was sealed off one Sunday as part of an organized *sanglier* drive. At intervals down the long dirt road, hunters had parked their vans, snout first, in the bushes. Figures in camouflage green—armed, immobile, and sinister—waited while their dogs circled and backtracked, collar bells clinking, their barking hoarse with excitement. I felt as though I had walked into a manhunt, or a war.

The first casualty appeared as I was nearing the house. A hunter was coming toward me with the sun directly behind him, and all I could make out in the distance was his silhouette. A rifle barrel slanted above one shoulder, and in his arms he was cradling something large, something with legs that flopped loosely on either side of the man's body as he walked.

He stopped when he reached me. The black and tan hound he was holding rolled a lugubrious eye at our dogs, and the hunter, no less mournful, wished me good morning. I asked after the hound's health. Had he been attacked and savaged in the bushes by an oversized piglet, a cornered *sanglier* protecting his patch?

"*Ah, le pauvre*," the hunter said. "He has passed all summer in the kennel, and that makes the paws soft. He's run too far this morning. His feet hurt."

By eleven-thirty, the road was empty again. The army had withdrawn, to regroup and change uniforms and weapons. Combat fatigues and guns were replaced by clean shirts and knives and forks in preparation for an assault on the table.

Sunday lunch, at any time of year, is my favorite meal.

The morning is undisturbed by work, the afternoon siesta free of guilt. I feel that restaurants have a more than usually good-humored air about them, almost an undercurrent of festivity. And I'm sure that chefs try harder, knowing their clients have come to enjoy the cooking rather than to discuss business. There's no doubt about it. Food tastes better on Sunday.

There are a dozen good restaurants within a twenty-minute drive of the house; spoiled for choice, we can pick a place that suits the weather. The Mas Tourteron, with its vast shady courtyard and a selection of straw hats to keep customers' heads cool, is as close as one gets to eating in heaven on a ninety-degree day. In the winter, there is the Auberge de l'Aiguebrun—an open fire, a high, light, white-curtained room, and the view of a private valley.

What sets these apart from most other local restaurants, and indeed from most other restaurants in France, is that in both cases the chefs are women. The traditional division of labor has always placed the man in front of the oven and Madame behind the till. Now times are beginning to change, although no female chef has yet come close in terms of national recognition to Alain Ducasse, who has enough Michelin stars to decorate a tree. Women in France are better represented in medicine, in politics, and in the law than they are in restaurant kitchens. I find this odd, and I wondered if chauvinism has had something to do with it.

There is only one man to consult over a tricky social question like this if you want a provocative answer: Régis, who excels—in fact, I believe he's been asked to represent France—in both gastronomy and chauvinism, and who is happy to share his opinions with the world. It didn't surprise me that he held strong views on the matter of female chefs, and when I asked him why there weren't more of them, the answer came out like a bullet. "What you have to understand," he said, "is that in France some things are considered too important to be left to women."

Female doctors, lawyers, and cabinet ministers Régis found curious but acceptable. Female chefs (and female sommeliers) made him suspicious and uneasy. It was somehow against the proper order of things. Professional cooking was man's work.

He ate his words one winter Sunday, during lunch at the Auberge de l'Aiguebrun. After a cautious start with a gratin of Swiss chard, he continued without any apparent difficulty to deal with a lamb stew, a small mountain of various cheeses, and a dark, dense slab of triple-strength chocolate in a puddle of *crème anglaise*—all cooked by a woman.

We stood outside the restaurant, and I waited for him to admit that he might have been wrong. Not a chance. He merely adjusted his chauvinism to suit the moment.

"Only in France," he said, "can you find cooking like that in the middle of nowhere." He waved an arm at the mountains and at the sun pouring into the funnel of the valley. "It's good to be back, isn't it?"

Yes, it's good to be back.

The Unsolved Murder of the Handsome Butcher

It was very nearly death at first sight when I met Marius. I saw his tall figure in the distance, his hands in his pockets, strolling along in the middle of the road that leads to the village. He heard the car engine and turned to look back, so he knew I was coming. But after one or two alarming experiences on that particular stretch of road, I had learned to distrust the unpredictable movements of pedestrians, bicyclists, tractor drivers, dogs, and confused chickens, and so I slowed down. Luckily for both of us, my foot was resting on the brake when he leaped in front of the car, arms stretched wide as though he wanted to embrace it. I stopped with about eighteen inches to spare.

He nodded at me before walking around to the passenger door and getting into the car. "*Bieng,*" he said in his familiar southern dialect. "You're going to the village. My Mobylette is being repaired."

He asked to be dropped off in front of the café. But when we got there he showed no sign of leaving the car, seemingly fascinated by the assortment of small change that I kept in a tray by the gearshift to feed parking meters.

"You wouldn't have ten francs, would you? For a phone call?"

I pointed to the tray. He sifted carefully through the coins, took a ten-franc piece, beamed at me, and disappeared into the café, without so much as a token glance at the pay phone he had to pass on his way in.

Over the next few weeks, a pattern emerged. Marius would appear on the horizon, patrolling the road or wandering through the village, his open arms demanding transport. His motorized bicycle would still be undergoing repairs, and he'd need to make another phone call. After a while, we abandoned the tiresome formalities. I would simply leave two ten-franc pieces in the tray by the gearshift; Marius would put them in his pocket. It was an efficient and civilized arrangement that suited us both, as neither of us liked to discuss money.

It must have been two or three months before our relationship progressed from low finance and began to take on some kind of social dimension. I went into the post office one morning, and there I found Marius engaged in a negotiation involving a scrap of paper, which he kept pushing toward Madame behind the counter. She kept shaking her head and pushing it back. There were many shrugs, and eventually an exchange of those audible pouts—air being expelled through downturned, disdainful lips—that the French like to use when indicating disapproval or disagreement. And then, silence. The negotiation had clearly foundered.

Madame used my arrival as an excuse to put an end to the proceedings, leaning around Marius to wish me good morning. When he turned and saw me, his expression changed from a scowl to a smile, and he clapped me on the shoulder. "I'll wait for you outside," he said.

The problem, as he explained it to me, was that Madame, whom he accused of having no imagination and a sour and unhelpful disposition, had refused to cash a check for five hundred francs—a valid financial instrument, he said, and held it up for inspection.

It flapped sadly in the wind as he passed it to me. I suppose the check might once have been legitimate, but now it was rumpled and grubby, the words and figures faded and almost indecipherable. It would have been an act of supreme optimism to part with any money in return for such a tattered and unconvincing relic. And besides, I told Marius, I didn't have five hundred francs on me.

"*Tant pis*," he said. "In that case, you can buy me a drink."

I find it hard to resist this kind of amiable effrontery, perhaps because I have very little of it myself, and so, two minutes later, Marius and I were sitting at a table in the back of the café. All our previous meetings had been in the car, when my eyes had been on the road; this was the first time I'd had a chance to take a close look at him.

His face was a study in the brutal effect that too much weather can have on the skin: a complexion like flayed meat, ruts where other faces would have wrinkles, wrinkles where other faces would be smooth. But the eyes were bright, and he had a full head of hair, cut *en brosse*, spiky and grizzled. I put his age at around sixty. He took a big box of kitchen matches from the pocket of his army surplus jacket and lit a cigarette. I saw that the first joint of his left index finger was missing, probably a slip of the pneumatic secateurs while he'd been pruning vines.

The first swallow of red wine went down, marked by a small shudder of appreciation, and he started to question me. I spoke French like a German, he said. He was surprised when I told him I was English, it being well known that the Englishman abroad prefers to stay within the familiar bounds of his own language, merely raising the volume of his speech to overcome any misunderstanding with the natives. Marius put his hands to his ears and grinned, his face collapsing into a web of creases.

But what was an Englishman doing here in the winter? What kind of work did I do? It was a question I had often been asked, and the answer invariably prompted one of two reactions. Either pity, since writing is a notoriously precarious occupation, or interest, sometimes even tinged with the respect that the French still have for anyone who labors in the arts. Marius was in the second category.

"Ah," he said, "*un homme de lettres*. But clearly not poor." He tapped his empty glass.

More refreshment arrived, and the questions continued. When I explained what it was that I liked to write about, Marius leaned forward, half-closing his eyes against the smoke from his cigarette, the picture of a man with confidential information to impart. "I was born here." He waved an arm in the general direction of his birthplace, somewhere outside the café. "There are stories I could tell you. But another time, not now."

He had a prior engagement. Apparently there was a funeral in the village that day, and he never missed funerals. He liked the measured pace of the funeral service, the solemnity, the music, the sight of the female mourners in their best clothes and high heels. And if the ceremony was to celebrate the burial of an old enemy, he liked it even more. The final victory, he called it, a testament to his own superior powers of survival. He reached over to seize my wrist and look at my watch. Time to go. Stories would have to wait.

I was disappointed. To hear a good Provençal storyteller is to hear a performance given by a master of the art of verbal embroidery, a prince of the pregnant pause, the shocked expression, and the belly laugh. Drama is extracted from the most mundane occasions—a trip to the garage, the gutting of a chicken, the discovery of a wasps' nest under the roof. Coming from the right person, these small moments can take on a dramatic significance more suited to the Comédie Française than a village bar, and I always find them fascinating.

The next time I saw Marius, he was crouched over his Mobylette at the side of the road, peering into the fuel tank, his head cocked in a listening position as though he were waiting for it to whisper in his ear. Dry as a rock in July, he said to me as he folded himself into the car. But I could take him to the garage to get a *bidon* of fuel, *non*? And then I could buy him a drink, as it had been an exasperating morning. There was, as usual with Marius, the confident assumption that I had no pressing plans of my own which might interfere with my duties as his emergency chauffeur.

We settled in the café, and I asked him if he had enjoyed his last funeral.

"*Pas mal*," he said. "It was old Fernand." He tapped the side of his nose. "You know? They say he was one of the five husbands. You must have heard the story."

When I shook my head, he turned to call for a carafe of wine. And then he began. He glanced at me from time to time for emphasis, or to see if I had understood, but for the most part his eyes stared off into the distance, examining his memory.

For some reason, he said, butchers and women often have this affinity, a closeness that goes beyond the simple transaction of buying and selling meat. Who knows why? It might be the sight of all that flesh, the pinkness of it, the slap it makes on the block, the promise of a choice cut. Whatever the reason, it is not unusual for a certain intimacy to develop between butcher and client. And when the butcher is young and good-looking there is often the added pleasure of a little flirtation over the lamb chops. This is normally as far as it goes, a harmless moment or two, something to bring a sparkle to a woman's eye as she goes about her daily business.

Normally, but not always. And not in the case of the butcher whom we shall call Arnaud. At the time the story takes place, many years ago, he was newly arrived in the village, having taken over when the old butcher, a glum, unsmiling man who was stingy with his meat, had retired. The local ladies were never quick with their opinions, but they gradually began to approve of Arnaud as news of what he was doing was broadcast from mouth to ear on the *téléphone arabe*. He transformed the little butcher's shop—repainting, replacing ancient fittings, installing modern lighting—and by the time he had finished it was a joy to go in there, to be greeted by gleaming steel and glass, the clean scent of fresh sawdust on the floor, and the smile of the young proprietor.

He, too, was a considerable change for the better, with his shining black hair and brown eyes. But what set him apart from most other men of his time were his teeth. In those days, rural dentists were few and far between, and their techniques ran more to extraction than repair. Consequently, it was rare to see an adult without a gap or two, and those teeth that had survived were often in a sad way—crooked, dingy, stained with wine and tobacco. The teeth of Arnaud, however, were startling in their perfection: they were white, they were even, they were all there. Women meeting him for the first time would come away dazzled, asking themselves why it was that such a *beau garçon* didn't appear to be married.

Arnaud was not unaware of the effect he had on his female clients. (Indeed, it came out later during the investigation that he had been obliged to leave his previous place of work in another village after some complications with the wife of the mayor.) But he was a businessman, and if smiling at his customers led to more business, he would smile. *C'est normal.*

It must be said also that he was a good butcher. His meat was properly hung and aged, his blood sausage and *andouillettes* plump and amply filled, his pâtés dense and rich. His cuts were generous, often a few grams more than had been asked for; never less. He even gave away marrow bones. Gave them away! And always, as he handed over the packages of neatly wrapped pink waxed paper printed with his name and the illustration of a jovial cow, there would be the sunburst of his smile.

All through that first winter and that first spring, his popularity grew. The men of the village found themselves eating more meat than they had eaten in the time of the old butcher, and better meat, too. When they mentioned this, their wives would nod. Yes, they would say, the new one is a great improvement. The village is lucky to have him. And some of the wives, as they looked across the table at their husbands and made an involuntary comparison, would catch themselves thinking about young Arnaud in a way that had very little to do with his professional skills. Those shoulders! And those teeth!

The trouble started at the end of June, with the beginning of the true heat. The village was built on a hill, and the stone buildings that faced full south seemed to suck up the sun and store it overnight. In private houses, shutters could be closed against the glare and the steadily rising temperature, but commercial establishments were not so fortunate. Their display windows invited the heat, and magnified it. And so Arnaud was obliged to modify his working methods to suit the climate. He cleared the window of anything perishable, replacing the usual arrangements of sausages and prepared cuts with a notice informing his clientele that his meat was being kept in the cool storage area at the back of the shop.

Naturally, the butcher himself needed some relief from the heat, and by early July Arnaud had adopted a more practical uniform than the canvas trousers and cotton sweater he usually wore. He still kept his *tablier,* the long white (although frequently bloodstained) apron that covered most of his chest and extended down to his shins. But beneath that he wore only a pair of old black cycling shorts, snug around the hips and buttocks, and rubber-soled clogs.

Business, already healthy, became even more brisk. Items hanging on the hooks behind the counter were suddenly much in demand, since to reach them Arnaud had to turn and stretch, exposing a muscular back and legs to the waiting customer. Expeditions to the cool area where the rest of the meat was kept were also very popular, involving, as they did, close proximity to an attractive and almost naked young man.

There were changes, too, in the appearance of Arnaud's customers. Everyday clothes and cursory grooming were replaced by summer dresses and makeup, even scent. The local hairdresser was kept unusually busy, and visitors to the village could be forgiven for thinking that the women they saw in the narrow streets were dressed for a fête. As for the husbands—well, those who noticed put it down to the weather. In any case, their wives were treating them well, with the extra attention that a touch of guilt often provokes, and feeding them like prizefighters in training. The husbands had no complaints.

July continued like an oven, one rainless, blistering day after another. Dogs and cats tolerated each other, sharing pools of shade, too stunned to squabble. In the fields, melons were coming to ripeness, the juiciest for years, and the grapes on the vines were warm to the touch. The village sprawled on its hilltop, stifling in a cocoon of hot, still air.

These were difficult days for the butcher, despite his flourishing business. He was finding that making friends in a small, closed community is a slow and cautious process. A newcomer—even a newcomer from a mere thirty kilometers away—is treated with guarded politeness in the street but excluded from the homes of his neighbors. He is on probation, often for several years. He is a foreigner; in Arnaud's case, a lonely foreigner.

To add to his problems, the demands of his business left him very little time to make the journey to Avignon, where the lights were brighter and social opportunities more promising. His working day started shortly after sunrise, when he would come down from his cramped apartment above the shop to swab the floor, sprinkle it with fresh sawdust, evict dead flies from the window, arrange his cuts, put an edge on his knives, and snatch a cup of coffee before his older customers, always the earliest, began to arrive just before eight. The hours between noon and two, while the rest of the world was taking its ease, were often spent picking up supplies. Wholesalers refused to deliver to the village; the streets were too narrow to accommodate their trucks. The afternoons were slow, early evenings the busiest. He was rarely able to close before seven, and then there was the gray torrent of paperwork: the day's receipts, suppliers' invoices, government forms requiring confirmation that the *code sanitaire* was being strictly observed, mutterings from the Crédit Agricole about his bank loan. It was a heavy burden for a man on his own. What he needed, Arnaud often told himself, was a wife.

He had one in early August, unfortunately not his own.

She was younger than most of his customers, and a good fifteen years younger than her husband. Her marriage, if not exactly arranged, had been vigorously promoted by the two sets of parents, whose vineyards occupied adjoining slopes below the village. What could be more satisfactory than a union of blood and earth, families and land? As each family made its discreet calculations, the savings on tractors, on fertilizer, on vine stock, and on labor became delightfully apparent. A date was set for the wedding, and the two principals were encouraged to become fond of each other.

The new husband, a placid man with modest ambitions, middle-aged from birth, found that marriage suited him. He was no longer dependent on his mother. He had someone to cook for him and mend his clothes and warm his bed on long winter nights. One day he would inherit both vineyards. There would be children. Life was good, and he was content.

But his young bride, once the excitement of the wedding was over, felt a sense of anticlimax that gradually turned into resentment as the reality of everyday routine set in. She was an only child and had been indulged. Now she was a wife, with a wife's responsibilities: a house to run, a budget to juggle, a husband who came home each night hungry, tired, caked in dust from the fields, happy to spend the evening with his boots off reading the newspaper. Happy to be dull. She looked into the future and saw a lifetime of work and tedium.

It was hardly surprising that she began to take increasing pleasure from her visits to the butcher, timing them for the afternoons when there was a greater chance that he would be alone. He was the bright spot in her day, always smiling and, she couldn't help but notice, a fine figure of a man in his abbreviated summer uniform—sturdy, unlike her scrawny husband, with a fine glow to his skin and a clump of thick black hair curling over the top of his apron.

It happened suddenly one afternoon, without anything being said. One minute they were standing side by side as he was wrapping some rump steak, close enough to feel the heat from each other's bodies; the next, they were upstairs in the little apartment, slippery with sweat, clothes on the floor.

Afterward, she let herself out of the shop, flushed and distracted, forgetting the meat on the counter.

Speculation is the hobby of a small village, and information seems to travel by osmosis, seeping into the consciousness as surely as sunlight through gauze. Secrets never last, and the women are always the first to know. In the weeks that followed his afternoon with the young wife, Arnaud noticed an increasing friskiness among his customers, and their tendency to stand closer to him. Hands that had previously been businesslike, paying money and receiving packages, now lingered, fingers brushing against his fingers. The young wife began to come in regularly just after two o'clock, closing the door behind her and turning the sign so that it read *Fermé*. Others followed, picking their moments. Arnaud lost weight and prospered.

It is not certain who first alerted the husbands. Perhaps one of the oldest women of the village, whose joy in life it was to denounce every irregularity she saw; perhaps one of the wives who was disappointed never to have made the hurried journey up the stairs to the dark, beef-scented bedroom. But, inevitably, gossip and suspicion grew, eventually reaching the husbands. Accusations were made in the privacy of the matrimonial bed. Denials were disbelieved. Finally, one husband confided in another, and he in another. They discovered that they were members of the same miserable club.

Five of them gathered one evening in the café: three farmers, the postman, and a man whose work for the insurance company often involved nights away from home. They took a table at the back away from the bar, a pack of cards disguising the true purpose of their meeting. In low, bitter voices, they told each other much the same story. She's changed. She's no longer the woman I married. That little *salaud* has destroyed our marriages, with his greasy smile and the obscenity of his shorts. As they sat there, the cards forgotten in front of them, their outrage feeding on pastis, their voices grew violent and loud. Too loud. The postman, the least fuddled head at the table, proposed another meeting, somewhere private, where they could talk about what was to be done.

By now it was nearing the end of September, and the hunting season had begun. And so they agreed to meet in the hills the following Sunday morning, five friends with their guns and dogs in search of the wild boar that caused such havoc rooting through the vineyards every autumn.

Within minutes of sunrise, Sunday was hot, more like July than September. By the time the five men reached the crest of the Luberon, their guns and bandoliers were weighing heavy on their shoulders, their lungs burning from the climb. They found shade beneath the branches of a giant cedar tree, eased their backs, passed a bottle around. The dogs explored the undergrowth by nose, following invisible zigzag paths as though they were being jerked along at the end of a cord, the bells on their collars chinking in the still air. There was no other sound, there were no other people. The men could talk undisturbed.

To punish the wives, or to punish the butcher?

A good beating, a few broken bones, his shop destroyed—that would teach him. Maybe, said one of the husbands. But he would recognize his attackers, and then the police would come. There would be questions, possibly jail. And who was to say it would stop him? Men recover from beatings. He would have the sympathy of the wives. It would start all over again. The bottle passed around in silence as the five men imagined living through long months, maybe more, in jail. If their wives were able to deceive them now, how much easier it would be when they were left alone. Finally, one of them said what they had all been thinking: It was necessary to find a permanent solution. One way or another, the butcher must go.

Only then would their lives and their wives return to the way they had been before this young goat had put them to shame.

The postman, always the most reasonable among them, was in favor of talking to him. Perhaps he could be persuaded to leave. Four heads shook in disagreement. Where was the punishment in that? Where was the revenge? Where was the justice? The village would laugh at them. They would spend the rest of their lives the target of whispers, the butt of jokes, five weaklings who stood by while their wives jumped in and out of another man's bed. Five men with horns and no guts.

The bottle was empty. One of the men got to his feet and placed it on a rock before coming back to pick up his gun and slide a cartridge into the breech. This is what we do, he said. Taking aim, he blew the bottle to fragments. He looked down at the others and shrugged. *Voilà.*

It was agreed, in the end, that they should draw straws to decide who was to carry out the sentence. When this had been done, the men went back down the mountain to have Sunday lunch with their wives.

The executioner chose the time with care, waiting for the dark of the moon, leaving the house when night was at its thickest. To be sure of a kill, he had loaded his gun with two shells of *chevrotine,* even though one blast of the heavy buckshot was enough to stop an elephant, let alone a man at arm's length. He must have wondered if the others were lying awake thinking of him as he went softly through the empty streets and up to the butcher's shop. And he must have cursed the time it took the butcher to come downstairs in response to the persistent tapping on his door.

He used both barrels, jammed up tight against the

butcher's chest, and didn't wait to see him fall. By the time lights started to go on in the neighboring houses, he was in the fields below the village, stumbling through the vines on his way home.

Sometime before dawn, the first gendarme arrived, roused from his bed by a call from one of the few telephones in the village. Half a dozen people were already standing in the pool of light spilling from the butcher's shop, horrified, fascinated, unable to keep their eyes away from the bloody carcass that lay just inside the door. Within an hour, a squad from Avignon was there to clear them away, remove the corpse, and set up an office in the *mairie* to begin the lengthy process of questioning the entire village.

It was a difficult time for the five husbands, a test of solidarity and friendship. They spent another Sunday morning in the forest, reminding each other that silence, total silence, was their only protection. Keep it behind the teeth, as one of them said, and nobody will ever know. The police will think it was an enemy from the butcher's previous life in another place, settling an old score. They passed the comforting bottle around and swore to say nothing.

Days passed, and then weeks—weeks without a confession, weeks without even a clue. Nobody admitted to knowing anything. And besides, there was a certain reluctance to discuss village affairs with outsiders in uniform. All the police were able to establish was the approximate time of death and, of course, the fact that the murderer had used a hunting rifle. Every man who held a *permis de chasse* was questioned, every rifle was carefully inspected. But unlike bullets, buckshot leaves no identifiable traces. The fatal shots could have come from any one of dozens of guns. The investigation eventually faltered, then stopped altogether, to become simply another dossier in the files. The village went back to work harvesting the grapes, which everyone agreed were exceptionally concentrated that year after a dry, warm autumn.

In time there was another butcher, an older, family man from the Ardèche who was happy to take over premises that were so well equipped, even down to the knives. He was pleasantly surprised to find himself welcomed with unusual friendliness by the men of the village.

"And that was the end of it," said Marius. "It must be nearly forty years ago now."

I asked him if the identity of the murderer had ever been established. There were, after all, at least five people who knew, and as he himself had said, keeping secrets in a village was like trying to hold water in your hand. But he just smiled and shook his head.

"I'll tell you this, though," he said, "everyone turned out the day they buried the butcher. They all had their reasons." He finished his wine, and stretched back in his chair. "*Beh oui.* It was a popular funeral."

New York Times Restaurant Critic Makes Astonishing Discovery: Provence Never Existed

The letter came from Gerald Simpson, a gentleman living in New York. He was puzzled by a piece he'd seen in the newspaper, which he had enclosed, and the article made sad reading. It condemned Provence as a region of clever peasants and bad food, and here was the source of Simpson's puzzlement. I don't remember it being like that at all, he wrote, when I was there on vacation. It's not like that in your books. What's happened? Can it have changed so much in the last few years?

I read the article a second time, and it did indeed make Provence sound unattractive and poorly served by its restaurants and food suppliers. I've been sent similar pieces before, written by journalists in search of what they like to think is a different angle. They are anxious to find what they call "the reality" that lurks behind the postcards of sunny lavender fields and smiling faces. Give them a disenchanted visitor, a surly shopkeeper, or a bad meal, and they go home happy; they have their story. I rarely agree with what they write, but that's fair enough. We all have our own ideas about Provence, and mine will inevitably differ from those of people who come for a week or two, particularly if they come during August, the most crowded, least typical month of the year.

The piece that I had been sent, "My Year in Provence Last August," appeared on April 22, 1998, in one of the world's most distinguished and influential newspapers, the *New York Times*. It was written by Ruth Reichl, whose name, I'm sure, causes a *frisson* of apprehension when it is dropped in the restaurant kitchens of Manhattan; more so during her tenure as restaurant reviewer for the *Times*, a position she no longer occupies but did that April. A shining beacon of gastronomic knowledge in a dim and ignorant world, a maker and breaker of culinary reputations—all in all, a woman who knows her onions, as one of those clever old peasants might say.

Not the least of Reichl's accomplishments as a food writer and editor is her ability to get to the heart of things without wasting a moment. In the course of her visit during August, she was able to investigate, consider, sum up, and dismiss an entire region of France—what diligence!— and yet still manage to find time to have a disappointing vacation.

What a catalogue of disappointment it was, too, from the very first breakfast: awful baguettes, worse croissants, sour coffee. A trip to the market failed to unearth a single ripe tomato. The peaches were hard as rocks. The green beans looked tired, and nothing makes a food critic's heart sink more quickly than the sight of a tired green bean. And the heart continued to sink. None of the potatoes had been grown in France. None of the butchers had any lamb. It was gourmet hell, and visits to the supermarket, where Reichl said she was forced to shop on nonmarket days, did nothing to temper her dissatisfaction. There, too, the food was pretty dreary. The meat and vegetables were a disaster. The cheeses came from factories. The bread was wrapped in plastic. And, horror of horrors, the selection of rosé wines alone took up more space than all the cereals, cookies, and crackers in her local D'Agostino market back home. Imagine such a thing! More wine than cookies! There can be few more telling signs than that of a society in the grip of depravity.

Other revelations will follow, but before they do it is worth examining the first part of this miserable litany in more detail. There is no doubt that you can find indifferent food in Provence, but to find it everywhere you look suggests carelessness or a profound lack of local knowledge. This would be understandable in the average tourist, but Reichl is anything but the average tourist. Her working life is devoted to the discovery of good food. She is doubtless extremely well connected in gastronomic and journalistic circles. She surely has friends or colleagues in France who could have told her that in Provence, as in the rest of the world, you need to know where to go. Didn't anyone give her a few good addresses? Didn't she ask for any? Didn't she read the excellent books of Patricia Wells, her counterpart at the *International Herald Tribune,* a food writer with an intimate and informed knowledge of Provence? Apparently not.

The elusive ripe tomato and the absence of lamb—two disappointments that we have never encountered during our years in Provence—might have been bad luck; or they might have been the result of arriving at the market and the butcher too late, when the best has already been bought. August is like that. As for the dreadful supermarket, it seems that again Reichl was either badly advised or not advised at all. Certainly there are supermarkets with factory cheese and plastic-wrapped bread, although I can't see why this was worth mentioning. Supermarkets are specifically designed to sell mass-produced food, much of which is legally obliged to come in plastic skin. Even so, not all supermarkets are alike. Plenty of them in Provence have fresh cheese and their own bakeries, even if the cookie selection may not be up to the D'Agostino standard.

In fact, most of the serious cooks we know use supermarkets only to stock up on basic commodities. They buy their meat, bread, oil, wine, and produce from small specialist shops, as their mothers used to do. And if they live in or near Avignon, they shop at Les Halles, one of the best food markets one could hope to find, in France or anywhere else. It's on the Place Pie, right in the center of town; not far, as it happens, from where Reichl was staying.

For twenty-five years, the market has provided a permanent outlet for local suppliers, and the forty stalls offer a stunning choice of meat, poultry, game, breads, cheeses, *charcuterie*, fruit, vegetables, herbs, spices, and oils—and a fish counter more than thirty yards long. Every weekday it opens at six and closes at noon. But parking is difficult in Avignon during August, and perhaps for that reason the market was ignored. A pity.

Never mind. If inspiration or the will to shop falter, there are always the local restaurants. Avignon has several which compare favorably with good New York restaurants—Hiely, L'Isle Sonnante, or La Cuisine de Reine are just three—but these somehow managed to elude the Reichl eye. Instead, we were told about a whimsical menu, read but not tasted, consisting of nothing but tomatoes. (Let us hope they were ripe.) This presumably prompted her remark about mediocre restaurants in major cities. It's enough to make you despair of keeping body and soul together during your stay in Provence.

But now, disillusioned and faint with hunger, we come to the most extraordinary revelation of all. Here it is in black and white, backed up by the considerable authority of the *New York Times*: "I had been dreaming of a Provence that never existed."

The sentence hit me with the force of an unripe tomato between the eyes, as you can imagine. Where had I been living all these years? And what about those other misguided writers? The Provence that Daudet, Giono, Ford Madox Ford, Lawrence Durrell, and M. F. K. Fisher knew and wrote about—the Provence that I know—doesn't exist. It never existed. It is a sunny figment of our imaginations, a romanticized fantasy.

I'm afraid that much of the blame for this monumental deception has to be laid at the door of a native son of Provence—alas, yet another overwrought and fanciful writer—Marcel Pagnol. Reichl is a keen admirer of his, and she shares her admiration with us: "The Provence I am most attached to is that of the great filmmaker Marcel Pagnol. It is a scratchy black-and-white world where men in cafés amuse themselves by hiding rocks under hats and waiting for someone to come along and kick them."

This, it seems to me, is like expecting contemporary America to resemble a Frank Capra movie set, but I felt that I should make some inquiries, and I cannot argue with the results. In fairness, I must report that hat-kicking, as a crowd-pleasing spectacle, has gone the way of the guillotine. A search through the archives in the mayor's office of my local village failed to reveal a single recorded instance of hats being kicked in public. When I asked the oldest man in the village bar if he had ever been amused by the kicking of hats, he looked at me sideways, took his drink and moved away. Even in the most remote villages of Haute Provence, where you might imagine coming across the odd, forgotten nest of hat-kickers, you are unlikely to find men in cafés amusing themselves with anything other than conversation, cards, or *boules*. First, bad food. Now this. Another dream shattered.

Nevertheless, there are visitors to Provence who seem able to look beyond fuzzy expectations and derive considerable enjoyment from what actually does exist. Unfortunately, they are tourists, and they are not welcome in Reichl's world. She prefers places that, in her words, are not quaint and not "touristed." Tourists, of course, are always other people; never us. We are different. We are *travelers*—intelligent, well-mannered, cultured, a blessing on our chosen destinations, a delight to have around. It's a common attitude, and one that I have always found condescending and offensive, as well as inaccurate. If you travel away from home for pleasure, you're a tourist, no matter how you like to dress it up. I consider myself a permanent tourist. Some of my best friends are tourists. Tourism makes an important contribution to the local economy and provides a living for many talented people—several cooks among them—who might otherwise have to look elsewhere to make ends meet.

Let's take, for example, the only two good restaurants Reichl was able to find in the whole of Provence: the Auberge de Noves and the Bistrot du Paradou. Both are excellent, as she says, and both are deservedly popular with tourists. Would they be able to sustain their standards if they had to depend on a purely local clientele? I very much doubt it.

There is a final note of disappointment even when describing the favored Bistrot du Paradou. The food was good, the ambience charming, and yet: "I sensed that there was something unreal about all this, an artful attempt to resurrect the spirit of Marcel Pagnol." Good grief! What could have provoked that? An outbreak of hat-kicking in the parking lot? The arrival of Charles Aznavour for lunch? Or the fact that the bistrot had only been in business for fifteen years and not fifteen generations? Whatever it was, it provided useful support for the theory of a nonexistent Provence.

The next Reichl vacation, so we're told, will be taken in Italy, that golden land of dreams, and I hope for her sake they all come true: waiters singing snatches of Puccini, lusty peasants treading the grapes with purple feet, glorious meals of hand-knitted pasta. *Buon appetito, signora!*

But now, for the benefit of my correspondent Mr. Simpson and any other brave souls who may still be considering a visit to Provence, here are a few good addresses—proof, I hope, that all is not lost. The addresses cover a fairly wide area, and so may involve your spending some time in the car with a map. But the countryside is beautiful, and what you find will be worth the trip. I should add that these are personal choices that have been made in my usual haphazard fashion over the years. They are in no way intended to be a complete and organized listing. One last warning: Addresses have a habit of changing, so it would be wise to check in the phone book or at the local Syndicat d'Initiative before you set off.

Markets

I have never found a more pleasant way to go shopping than to spend two or three hours in a Provençal market. The color, the abundance, the noise, the sometimes eccentric stall-holders, the mingling of smells, the offer of a sliver of cheese here and a mouthful of toast and *tapenade* there—all of these help to turn what began as an errand into a morning's entertainment.

An addict could visit a different market every day for several weeks, and this selection, which is best read with map to hand, is far from comprehensive. But I think it's enough to show that there is no such thing as a nonmarket day in Provence.

Monday: Bédarrides, Cadenet, Cavaillon, Forcalquier
Tuesday: Banon, Cucuron, Gordes, St. Saturnin-d'Apt, Vaison-la-Romaine
Wednesday: Cassis, Rognes, St. Rémy-de-Provence, Sault
Thursday: Cairanne, Nyons, Orange
Friday: Carpentras, Châteauneuf-du-Pape, Lourmarin, Pertuis
Saturday: Apt, Arles, Manosque, St.-Tropez
Sunday: Coustellet, L'Isle-sur-Sorgue, Mane

Wine

Here we are on delicate ground. One of the changes that has taken place in the Luberon over the past few years has been an enormous improvement in the quality of the *petits vins*. Small local vineyards are producing better and better wine; perhaps not of the same weight and complexity as the big vintages of Châteauneuf-du-Pape, but well made, easy to drink, and inexpensive. There are dozens of these wines, and that's the problem. It would take a greater thirst than mine to try them all, and I'm sure that I have omitted several treasures. Further research is being carried out on a daily basis. Meanwhile, here are a few favorites.

Château La Canorgue, Bonnieux
Reds and whites are good, and there is a wonderfully pale, smoky rosé, most of which is bought by local restaurants. To ensure getting a case or two, you need to go to the château in March or April.

Domaine Constantin-Chevalier, Lourmarin
Somehow, two men and their tractors manage to take care of about fifty acres of vines. The wines, particularly the reds, are beginning to gather medals and appear on restaurant wine lists. If this continues, there is a good chance that the staff will be increased to three.

Domaine de La Royére, Oppède
The only vineyard I know where the winemaker is a woman, and very good she is, too. Anne Hugues turns the grapes into excellent wines, while her hus-

band makes a fine *marc,* potent and deceptively smooth. Drive with caution after a tasting.

Château La Verrerie, Puget-sur-Durance
An ancient vineyard, replanted and completely rejuvenated by a wine-loving businessman with the help of Jacky Coll, one of the region's most accomplished architects of the grape. His touch has produced some exceptional reds.

Domaine de La Citadelle, Ménerbes
One of the bigger local properties, and the home of a corkscrew museum as well as a wide and interesting range of Côtes du Luberon. Tasting sessions tend to be prolonged and sometimes convivial.

La Cave du Septier, Apt
Not a vineyard, but a shop run by Hélène and Thierry Riols, who know all that I wish I knew about the wines of Provence. Put yourself in their hands, and drink what they recommend. Naturally, as responsible wine merchants, they also stock all kinds of splendid bottles from Bordeaux and Burgundy. However, since these come from foreign parts they need not concern us here.

Olive Oil

Probably the most fashionable Provençal oils are those from the valley of Les Baux, and if you happen to be near Maussane-les-Alpilles just after the olives are gathered toward the end of the year, you can find those oils in the tiny Maussane cooperative. But the oils go quickly, and summer visitors are likely to have better luck farther north in Haute Provence.

Here, on the outskirts of Mane, you will find Oliviers & Co., a shop that sells a remarkable range of handpicked oils from the Mediterranean basin—Italy, Greece, Sicily, Corsica, Spain—as well as some of the best homegrown oils. Take a baguette into the shop with you, because you can taste before you buy. (Porcelain tasting spoons are provided, but you can't beat the combination of good oil on fresh bread.) And while you're there, pick up some olive oil soap, which is said to impart a Mediterranean glow to the complexion.

Honey

Every market has its honey stand, and you may one day bump into my favorite honey salesman, Monsieur Reynaud. "My bees," he will tell you, "have flown in from Italy to make this honey." This, for some reason, I find very impressive, and so there is almost always a pot of Reynaud honey in the house.

But if you should want to see what the local bees can do, go to the Mas des Abeilles, on the Claparèdes plateau above Bonnieux. You'll find honey flavored with lavender, with rosemary, or with thyme; honey vinegar; royal jelly; and a delicious honey mustard. As a bonus, there's a bee's-eye view of Mont Ventoux and the Luberon.

Bread

As with practically everything edible in France, there are pronounced and often noisy differences of opinion about what constitutes the perfect texture and even the perfect form of your daily bread. The *fougasse,* the *boule,* the *pain fendu,* the *restaurant, pain de campagne, pain au levain*—each has its own ardent lobby. Bakeries are subject to the same highly subjective judgments, and these recommendations are therefore a matter of purely personal taste.

Boulangerie Georgjon, in Rognes
This has perhaps the most enticing smell, a warm, buttery welcome as you step into the shop. As well as bread, the baker makes his own almond biscuits, two distinct types of croissant, and tarts with a seductive, fruity glaze. All are good.

Boulangerie Testanière, in Lumières
Here is bread with a dense, slightly more chewy texture than the normal baguette. It is very popular with local residents, and if you don't get in early on Sunday morning the shelves will be bare.

Boulangerie Arniaud, in Rustrel
The decor has scarcely changed since 1850. Nor, I imagine, has the taste of the bread—solid, filling, and satisfying, as bread should be. A *fougasse* rubbed with oil and sea salt and eaten with fresh tomatoes is a meal.

Auzet, in Cavaillon
Offers more varieties than I ever believed possible. The Auzets, *père et fils,* offer a menu of breads and, as long as they're not too busy, advice on what to eat with them.

Cheese

Provence is not a land of lush pastures, and a cow, so they say, is as rare as a genial tax inspector. But the goat flourishes in the scrub and the mountains, and goat cheeses are surprisingly versatile. When fresh, they are light, mild, and creamy. They become firmer with age, and more pungent when marinated in oil with herbs, rolled in coarse black pepper, or garnished with wild savory. I have seen them no bigger than a thimble—*petits crottins*—or in plump wedges as *camembert de chèvre,* but they normally come in discs about an inch thick and three inches across, often wrapped in dried chestnut leaves and tied with raffia. The farmers around Banon, in Haute Provence, produce the best-known cheese, but they have worthy competition throughout the Vaucluse.

Genevieve Molinas, in Oppede, makes the full range: dry or fresh, with pepper, with savory, *à la cendre* (cooked in embers), and *en camembert.*

Not far away, in Saignon, is the Ferme Auberge Chez Maryse, where you can buy the cheeses of Maryse Rouzière and also sample her cooking.

And at Les Hautes Courennes, in St.-Martin-de-Castillon, you can have probably your first taste of *cabrichon.*

For a wider selection of different cheeses, there is the excellent Fromagerie des Alpes in Cavaillon, where the cow and the ewe are represented as well as the goat. The cheeses are kept in beautiful condition, and the proprietors will be happy to guide you in your choice.

Chambres d'Hôtes

There are very few large hotels in rural Provence, and if current building restrictions remain in force it is unlikely there ever will be. But more and more private houses are offering simple, comfortable accommodation, a decent dinner, and the chance to meet the French at home. Three examples:

In Bonnieux, there is Le Clos du Buis, run by the Maurins. Below Ménerbes, Muriel and Didier Andreis have recently opened Les Peirelles. And in Saignon, Kamila Regent and Pierre Jaccaud have converted an old house in the center of the village. Don't expect to find room service or cocktail lounges. But the welcome will be friendly, you won't go hungry, and your hosts will be able to steer you to other good local addresses, from restaurants to vineyards.

Restaurants

There are enough to fill a book, and it's been written by a professional gastronomic correspondent, Jacques Gantié. The *Guide Gantié* describes 750 *bonnes tables* from one end of Provence to the other. Read it and eat.

Looking back through this list, I see great gaps. For these, I apologize. Where is the prince of butchers, the reliable truffle supplier, the sausage-maker extraordinaire? Who should you go to see for the definitive melon or the most succulent snail, the *petit-gris de Provence?* Who has the tastiest *tapenade?* There is no doubt that they exist, these gastronomic specialists who spend their lives helping to make our meals memorable. But Provence covers a large area, and I have only been exploring it for ten years or so. The longer I am here the more I realize I don't know.

One thing I do know is that if you're prepared to spend a little time looking and listening, your appetite will be rewarded. I would agree that the ingredients and flavors that form Provençal cuisine are distinct and particular, and not to everyone's taste. I happen to like them, and with the notable exception of tripe, which I've never been able to embrace with any real enthusiasm, I have found very little to complain about. To say that you can't eat well here is nonsense. To say that you need to devote some time and effort to do it is quite true. But that, so I've always believed, is part of the appreciation and true enjoyment of good food.

Recipe for a Village

I remember once being told that the annual rainfall in Provence is much the same as London's, although it arrives in more concentrated bursts. Looking out through the window, it seemed as though a six-month supply was being delivered all at once, a slanting gray curtain, thrumming against the tin tables on the terrace and dribbling off the chairs to trickle under the door before coming to rest in grubby puddles on the tiled floor.

The woman behind the bar lit another cigarette and blew smoke at her reflection in the mirror that hung above the row of bottles, pushing her hair back behind her ears and practicing her Jeanne Moreau pout. Radio Monte-Carlo's hysterical good humor fought a losing battle with the mood of the room. The café, normally half-filled with workmen from the local *chantiers* by this time in the early evening, was reduced to three damp customers. Two men and myself, prisoners of the weather, were waiting for the downfall to stop.

"It never rains like this in my village," I heard one of them say. "Never."

The other man sniffed, dismissing this meteorological curiosity. "The trouble with your village," he said, "is the drains."

"*Bof.* Better than having a mayor who's always drunk."

The display of micropatriotism continued, each man defending his village and disparaging the other's. Abuse and slander were heaped on everyone and everything. The butcher sold horse meat disguised as sirloin. The war memorial was disgracefully maintained. The street lamps were the ugliest in France, the inhabitants the surliest, the garbage collectors the laziest.

All this and worse went back and forth between the two men with a surprising lack of passion. Disagreements in Provence tend to be energetic and heated affairs; arms and voices are raised, the names of ancestors are invoked, tables are banged, chests are prodded. But everything I overheard—even a most inflammatory remark concerning the postman's wife—was muttered rather than bellowed. The two men might have been university professors debating the finer points of philosophy. I can only think that the rain had cooled their blood.

When I left the café to make a run for the car, they were still at it, nipping away at each other, determined to disagree. I knew both the villages that featured in this tribal squabble, and to an outsider like myself—with no intimate knowledge of the mayor's fondness for alcohol or the proclivities of the postman's wife—they didn't appear to be nests of vice and neglect. On the surface, at any rate, there was nothing about either of them to sustain a prolonged argument. But after talking to various friends and acquaintances over the next few days, it became clear that villages inspire highly partisan feelings.

A single trivial incident can set things off. All it takes is some kind of slight, real or imagined: a snub in the *boulangerie,* a workman taking his time to move his truck from a blocked alleyway, the baleful stare of an old woman as you walk by—these have all been quoted to me as proof that a village is *fermé,* cold and unwelcoming. On the other hand, should the inhabitants be friendly, talkative, and generally forthcoming, you'd better watch out. This is just a cloak for nosiness, and before you know it details of your private business will be pinned up on the notice board of the *mairie.*

The basic matter of location, in the eyes of many people, can damn a village without any help from the inhabitants. Too high, and there is no protection from the mistral, a well-known cause of bad temper and various minor insanities. Too low, and the streets are suffused by a permanent chilly gloom which, as village experts will tell you, is responsible for winter epidemics of flu, or even more disastrous afflictions. Why, it was only five hundred years ago that the population was almost wiped out by the plague. *Beh oui.*

The problems continue with architecture—"the whole place was ruined by the *salle des fêtes* they put up"—with not enough shops or with too many shops, with nowhere to park or with a parking area that dominates the village, with infestation by Parisians or deserted streets. In other words, as I was repeatedly told, there is no such thing as the ideal village.

One of the consolations of the short but often sharp

Provençal winter is that the days are less distracting. Guests are far away, biding their time until the warm weather arrives. Domestic chores are confined to keeping the fire supplied with logs and refilling the emptiness of the wine cellar after the ravages of summer. The garden is rock-hard and dormant, the pool is under its clammy cover, and the social round of the Luberon is, in our case, restricted to the occasional Sunday lunch. There is time to reflect on the mysteries of life, and I found myself wondering about and eventually constructing in my mind the ideal village.

Parts of it exist, although inconveniently scattered around in other villages, and so I have stolen those I like and brought them together. Most of my featured inhabitants exist as well. But in transplanting them I thought it only fair to give them disguises, and names have been changed to protect the guilty. The name of the village, St.-Bonnet-le-Froid, I chose because St. Bonnet is one of the more neglected saints in the religious calendar who doesn't even seem to have his own saint's day. So I've given him one (which officially belongs to St. Boris) to call his own: the second of May, just as summer is about to start.

St.-Bonnet is set on the top of a hill about ten minutes from our house, close enough so that the bread is still warm when I get back from the baker's in the morning. Not too close, though, because even in the imagined perfection of this ideal village, tongues will wag. More from curiosity than malice, they will wag about every aspect of daily life, and since we are foreigners, our daily lives would be more closely observed than most. Our guests, in their annual progress from pink to bronze, would be studied as closely as the postcards they send home. Our household's consumption of wine, revealed by the empty bottles, would be noted with admiration or dismay, but it would be noted. My wife's weakness for acquiring dogs would be quickly recognized, and rewarded with puppies that were surplus to requirements or vintage beagles too old to hunt. From the purchase of a new bicycle to the color of paint on the shutters, nothing would escape the village eye. More of this later.

One of the first essentials of any properly equipped village is a church. I considered the Abbaye de Sénanque, near Gordes, which is magnificent but a little intimidating and, I decided, far too big. I wanted something on a smaller scale, although of similar historical interest, and so my first theft would be to steal the church from St. Pantaléon. It is tiny and beautiful, with tombs cut into the rock on which the eleventh-century building stands. The tombs are now empty and—since they were made to accommodate eleventh-century-sized people—seem very small. The giants of today wouldn't fit, and they would need a separate, more capacious cemetery. Following tradition, this would enjoy the finest view in the village, the theory being that the occupants have all eternity to appreciate it.

But there would be other views for the rest of us, almost as good, toward the west for the sunset, and north to Mont Ventoux. The fields at the foot of the mountain are fertile, almost lush, with vines and olive and almond trees; its crest, in the summer, looks prematurely white with snow. In fact, this is not the remains of a freak blizzard; it's bare, bleached limestone, but when the sun catches it in the evening it has the rosy softness of a cushion. And there is no better place to watch the fade of light and the gradual creep of shadows across the mountain's face than the terrace of the village café.

If a Frenchman were to tell you of the many contributions his country has made to civilized life (and he doesn't take much persuading), the café would probably appear somewhere at the bottom of the list, if at all. It is an institution he has grown up with, a convenience he takes for granted. There is always a café. But ask visitors from Britain and America what appeals to them about France, and sooner or later—after the countryside, the culture, the food, or whatever else is their principal interest—most of them will say, often quite wistfully: "Of course, the French are so lucky to have cafés."

It's true that the British and the Americans have their bars, their pubs, their coffee shops, and their diners, even their carefully accessorized versions of the authentic French café, complete with aperitif posters from the 1920s, yellow Ricard ashtrays, sandwiches made with baguettes, and newspapers hanging on sticks. France, however, is where you find the real thing, the particular combination of sounds and traditions and services, the atmosphere which has evolved over centuries. That, not the decor, is what makes a café a café. Obviously, there are enormous variations: The Deux Magots in Paris would seem to have very little in common with a village café in the Luberon. And yet there are one or two very basic similarities.

First, you are left alone; sometimes, I must admit, for longer than you might want if the waiter is feeling liverish and antisocial. Once you've ordered, though, you have rented your seat for as long as you wish to occupy it. Nobody will hover over you waiting for you to have another one or get out. You are expected to linger. You can read a newspaper, write a love letter, daydream, plan a coup d'état or use the café as an office and run your business undisturbed. I knew a Parisian who used to arrive at La Coupole each morning at nine o'clock sharp with his briefcase and spend the entire working day at one of the tables in the front, overlooking the Boulevard du Montparnasse. I always envied him having an office with waiters and a fifty-foot bar. In those days, before the cell phone, cafés would take calls for their regular clients, making excuses or arranging rendezvous as instructed. Some, I hope, still do, because the idea of having an answering service that provides refreshments deserves to endure.

Another wonderful amenity provided by every good café, regardless of size, is free entertainment of the old-fashioned, nonelectronic kind. Sit for long enough, pretending to read, and you will be treated to an amateur variety show. The cast will be mainly local, with occasional guest appearances by visitors. (These are the customers who sit politely, waiting to be served. Locals are more likely to bawl their orders as they come through the door; or, when their habits become sufficiently well known, a grunt and a nod will be enough to bring them their usual tipple.) If, like me, you find people more interesting than television, then here, as a fly on the café wall, is the place to watch them.

First to arrive, while the floor is still wet from its morning swabbing, are those battered ornaments of the local construction business, the masons. Their voices have the rasp that comes from cigarettes and the dust of a hundred demolitions. Their clothes and boots already look as though they've done a day's work. Their hands are meaty, with muscular fingers and sandpaper skin from juggling with two-hundred-pound blocks of stone. Their faces are raw in the winter, seared in the summer. Amazingly, they are almost always good-humored, despite brutal and frequently hazardous working conditions. When they leave, taking their noise with them, the café seems unnaturally still.

But quite soon their place is taken by the professional men, neat in their jackets and pressed trousers, briefcases loaded for a day at the desk in Apt or Cavaillon. They are a subdued contrast to the boisterous masons, serious and preoccupied with the cares of commerce. They check their watches frequently, make notes on small pads of what looks like graph paper, and brush their laps free of croissant crumbs after every mouthful. You know that their offices will be extremely tidy.

The first woman of the day is the owner of a hairdressing salon in a nearby village. Her hair is the color of the moment, somewhere between dark henna and aubergine, cut short. She will have spent a great deal of time tousling it to her satisfaction before leaving home. Her complexion glows with a radiance that is a credit to the house of Lancôme, and she is extraordinarily wide-eyed and vivacious for such an early, bleary hour. She orders a *noisette* coffee with a dash of milk, holding the cup with her aubergine-tipped pinky extended as she studies the lead story in *Allo!* magazine and wishes she could get her hands on the Duchess of York's hair.

Her departure, on small, glistening feet, signals the start of a quiet period. It's still too early for alcohol, except for the driver of the truck bringing beer supplies. He'll have a businesslike glass—but only to satisfy himself that the beer has the correct, chilled bite—after he's unloaded the kegs. He rumbles off, wiping his mouth with the back of his hand, leaving the café to prepare for the second shift of the morning. Tables are cleared, glasses are polished, the wave bands of the radio are explored in an effort to escape a numbing attack of French rap music.

Eventually, business picks up again. Two figures, nodding politely, make a tentative entrance and sit with their guidebooks by the window. They wear the uniform of prudent tourists: anoraks, in case of a sudden change in the weather, and those abdominal growths designed to confuse pickpockets—pouches of black nylon strapped around their waists, pregnant with valuables. After a moment of hesitation, they order glasses of wine, looking a little guilty as they toast each other.

Midmorning may be early for them, but it certainly isn't for the quartet of village elders, with a collective age of more than three hundred years, who arrive next. Tumblers of pink wine are brought to them, and the cards for *belote*. But before they start to play, four heads in flat caps swivel on tortoise necks to inspect the strangers. They are from the pre-tourist generation, the old men, often puzzled by the popularity of Provence, sometimes pleasantly surprised at the prices their disused barns and scrubby, unproductive patches of land can fetch: quarter of a million francs for a ruin, half a million or more for a modest house. And then another small fortune spent on indoor sanitation and central heating. *Putaing*, how the world has changed.

While the four musketeers get on with their cards, it's time to meet one of the café's main attractions, *madame la patronne*, a woman of a certain age with a taste for hoop earrings the size of a parrot's perch and precipitous décolletage. I've stolen her from a bar in Marseille, where I watched her presiding over her territory in a pair of conspicuously tight tigerskin trousers, dispensing drinks, sympathy, and insults to a group of regulars. Now there, I thought to myself, is a woman born to run a café. And, by a happy coincidence, her name was Fanny.

The relevance of her name is linked to the *boules* court under the trees by the side of the terrace, another stolen attraction. (You can see the original court next to the Lou Pastre Café in Apt.) Every day, weather permitting, the spectators—experts to a man—settle on a low stone wall to offer their opinions on the performance of the players, and the version of the game being played is *pétanque*. This was invented, perhaps accidentally, in La Ciotat nearly a hundred years ago. Until then, the style of play had been a running throw, but on this eventful day, one of the players stood still when he threw, his feet together, or *pieds tanqués*. Was it fatigue, idleness, an ingrowing toenail, or arthritis? Whatever the reason, it caught on, and the new technique was then used regularly on the court outside the local bar.

And who was behind the bar? None other than the original Fanny, a lady of considerable charms and a sweet, accommodating nature. If, in the course of a game, one of the players should be in despair after a terrible run of luck, he would leave the court, go into the bar, and collect his consolation prize: a kiss from Fanny. In time, this became part of the vocabulary of *boules*. Today, if you should hear one of the men on the wall sigh and say, *"Té, il a encore baisé Fanny,"* he's not making a romantic observation, but commenting on the player's failure to score. Not long ago, I saw a set of *boules* displayed in a shop window that were so technologically advanced, so perfectly weighted, that they were guaranteed to be *"Anti-Fanny."*

The influence of the modern Fanny, chatelaine of my imaginary café, extends far beyond the bar and the *boules* court. More, much more, than an occasional consolation prize, she is the nearest thing the village has to a resident psychiatrist, a patient listener to the dreams and woes of her customers, a provider of spiritual and alcoholic encouragement. She also acts as unofficial banker, offering credit and even making modest loans to deserving and trustworthy cases. And, in return for these comforts and services, she receives generous transfusions of the lifeblood of the village: gossip. Feuds, domestic battles, illicit liaisons, lottery windfalls—she hears about them all. She is careful to edit the news before passing it on, and to protect her informants. Like a journalist who will only make a discreet reference to a source close to the President, she never reveals the author of the latest leak; *on dit* is as close as she gets. But that's usually enough to send rumor—the invisible inhabitant of every village—scuttling through the streets like a dog after a ball.

With a few exceptions, all the adults of the village make a daily stop at the café. One of them is almost a fixture, always on the same stool at the end of the bar just inside the entrance, perfectly placed to ambush the unwary as they enter. It is Farigoule, the retired schoolteacher, who has been working on a book (although, given his constant presence at the bar, one wonders when) ever since he gave up academic life eight years ago. The café is his classroom and you, unless you're very fast on your feet coming through the door, will be his pupil.

He is a one-man Académie Française, dedicated to the preservation of the French language and loudly indignant about what he calls the Anglo-Saxon contamination of his mother tongue, among many other modern tragedies. His current favorite horror—I should probably call it his *bête noire*—is the malign and seemingly irresistible influence of Hollywood. Farigoule's considered opinion is that the film industry is merely a front for cultural espionage directed against France. He will, however, admit to having gone to see *Titanic* (more out of a secret admiration for Leonardo DiCaprio's cheekbones, if you believe Fanny, than any interest in the story). When asked what he thought of the film, his review was short but favorable: "The ship sank and nearly everyone perished. Most enjoyable."

A close runner-up to Farigoule in regular attendance at the café is Tommi, the village expatriate. Originally from a distant, Scandinavian country, he has worked hard over the years to transform himself into a French peasant. He is probably the last man in the village to smoke unfiltered Gauloises, and has mastered the peasant's knack of leaving the final quarter of an inch screwed into the corner of his mouth so that it bobs up and down on his lower lip when he speaks. Pastis is his drink, which he always refers to as *pastaga,* and he carries an Opinel pocket knife which he uses to cut up the *steack frites* he orders every day at noon, tapping its wooden handle on the table to release its ancient, blackened blade. Who would think he came from a nice middle-class family in Oslo?

Tommi has appointed himself an intermediary—a kind of shuttle diplomat—in the long-running vendetta between the brothers Vial, who own adjoining properties in the valley below the village. Dark, stringy men with the narrow faces of whippets, they haven't spoken to each other for twenty years. Nobody knows for sure what started the feud. It might have been disappointment over an inheritance, a dispute over water or a woman, or simply a mutual dislike that has turned into an enjoyable loathing. The two Vials sit at opposite ends of the café, getting up from time to time to leave accusations and insults with Tommi, who passes them on with conciliatory shrugs, nodding gravely at the response. Back he goes to the other brother. It's known locally as the waltz of the three wise men.

For light relief, the café regulars rely on the turbulent love life of Josette, the baker's daughter, a girl whose emotional state can be gauged by her wardrobe the moment she comes through the door. If the current romance is flourishing, she saunters in on platform heels wearing a microscopic skirt, with a crash helmet swinging like a trophy from one hand. Perched on a bar stool, she waits for Lothario to arrive on his *moto*, whispering to Fanny in between giggles and lipsticked sips of a Perrier *menthe*. But if the course of true love has taken a temporary dive, skirt and heels are replaced by dungarees and espadrilles, giggling by shuddering sighs, and Fanny has to dig around behind the bar to find a paper napkin for the tears.

Unmoved by affairs of the heart—unless, of course, the heart should stop beating and provide the excuse for another burial—is Marius. For him, I would like to create an official post in the village hierarchy—*entrepreneur de pompes funèbres*, or resident funeral director. This might help to give a semblance of authority to his hobby, but he would have to learn to be more subtle in his exchanges with his future clients, particularly Jacky, the oldest of the old men playing cards at the next table.

"*Eh, mon vieux*, how are you feeling today?"

"*Ça va, ça va.* I'm well."

"Pity."

This is enough to make a sensitive man take umbrage and go somewhere else to die, but with a little coaching I feel certain that Marius could disguise his natural enthusiasm for what he calls the final celebration. And he would have to give up his plans to start the ultimate sweepstakes. Runners, if you could call them that, would be everyone in the village over sixty-five. Bets would be placed on their longevity, and winners paid after the funeral, cash on the gravestone. Marius takes the view that this is no more macabre than life insurance, with the added bonus of instant reimbursement.

You may have noticed by now that there is an imbalance between the sexes here, with the male customers greatly outnumbering the females. Where are the ladies of St.-Bonnet?

The different generations keep away from the café for different reasons. The younger women work, and when they're not working they're at home cleaning the house, paying the bills, chasing the children to bed, and cooking dinner for the senior child, the husband, who has stopped off in the café until it's safe to go home.

The elder village ladies have two problems with the café. The first is Fanny, whom they consider *dragueuse,* a little too flirtatious and frisky for their taste, with a little too much bosom on public view. The second is that they can perform their function as an unofficial watch committee far more efficiently if they are on duty in the small square at the entrance to the village. Installed on chairs outside the house of their commander in chief, the widow Pipon, everything is within range of their radar: the post office, the *boulangerie,* the café, the parking lot, the *mairie,* and the church. They have long ago abandoned any pretense that they are simply taking the air, although a few of them may have some token scraps of knitting in their laps. They are there to observe and comment on everybody's business.

The most insignificant change in daily routine is cause

for speculation. A young housewife buying more bread than usual must mean guests. Who are they? A confirmed heretic paying a visit to the church must have something juicy to confess. What is it? A local real estate agent pulls up in his mafia-black Land Cruiser and ducks into the *mairie,* clutching documents. Whose house is he trying to get his hands on? And—*mon dieu!*—the tourists. These young girls are wearing lingerie on the street! They might as well be naked! Here in the middle of St.-Bonnet-le-Froid, a respectable village! In the absence of anything else to titillate their curiosity, the old ladies can always fall back on the drinking habits of the men in the café, Josette's amours—"She'll come to a bad end, that one"—or old, unconfirmed, and therefore delightfully possible rumors.

The watch committee is part of the family that you have to be prepared to adopt if you choose to live in a tiny, curious community, and that is one of the drawbacks of village life. We once tried it, many years ago, and the memories of our first few days are still fresh in my mind. We had barely moved in when the spinster sisters who were our neighbors appeared on the doorstep demanding a tour of inspection. They looked everywhere and wanted to know the price of everything. How fortunate we were, they said, to have a telephone, one of the few in the village. The next morning their brother arrived, made the calls he'd been saving up for the past three months, and left fifty centimes on the table by the phone.

We put up with this and all that followed because we were foreigners desperately anxious not to cause offense. We had chosen to live with these people, after all. They hadn't chosen us.

Village life taught us early on that what you gain in

companionship and convenience you lose in privacy. The face at the window and the knock on the door can come at any time, and there's no escape. You can hide, but you can't run. *They know you're in there.* They know because your shutters are open, and nobody leaves a house without closing the shutters. (You can, of course, always fool them by closing the shutters and staying at home, but then you'd be spending your life in the dark.) Your movements are monitored, your mail examined, your habits discussed and analyzed.

I'm sure this isn't confined to France. Go to live in the Hebrides or Vermont or a hamlet outside Munich; you will find the same fascination with newcomers, and you'll be considered newcomers for a good five or ten years. It's obvious that many people enjoy this, but I've discovered that I don't. I like to come and go without having to explain, every fifty yards, what I'm doing. I like a little privacy in my private life. That is why for me, a village—even St.-Bonnet-le-Froid, my ideal village—is best enjoyed at a distance. It will always be a great place to visit. But I wouldn't want to live there.

Curious Reasons
for Liking Provence

Driving along the back roads of the Vaucluse, you cannot help noticing the high proportion of cars that are well past the first flush of youth. With their mottled, rusty complexions, engines in the final stages of bronchitis, and exhaust pipes adangle, they seem to last almost as long as their owners, kind and good souls who are obviously prepared to put up with their cars' mechanical idiosyncrasies. When we first came to live here, I assumed that this loyalty to old iron sprang from the frugal nature of the inhabitants and their reluctance to part with any piece of machinery, no matter how ramshackle, while it could still be kicked or coaxed into life. Then we bought a car, and I understood.

Frugality has nothing to do with the Provençal motorist's attachment to his limping '71 Citroën or the exhausted Peugeot with 400,000 kilometers on it. Shortage of funds is not the problem here. The reason for all those disreputable old bangers on the roads, I'm convinced, is that the process of buying a new car is often so infuriating, so frustrating, and so time-consuming that if you have any sense you never wish to repeat it. As we discovered, it is not enough—not *nearly* enough—to have a valid driver's license and a check. The buyer is also required to prove that he or she officially exists, and don't think you can do this simply by waving your passport under the nose of authority. Other documents are demanded (usually one at a time, so that you have to keep coming back) to prove that your driver's license, your checkbook, and your passport are not just artful counterfeits. For some reason, phone and electricity bills are considered to be exempt from the forger's attentions, and these, together with a handful of old envelopes addressed to you, will eventually do the trick. But it can be a long and weary journey, demanding much stamina and patience. Or so it was when we were obliged to go through it seven or eight years ago.

Things will have changed, I told myself, when the time came to replace our car. This is the New Europe, blazing along in a white-hot streak of multinational cooperation and efficiency, with factories spewing out hundreds of thousands of cars each year. These cars had to be sold. Big business was on my side. And even if it wasn't, even if things hadn't changed, I was no longer an innocent in these matters. I knew what to expect, and when I arrived at the showroom I was fully prepared, confident that the comprehensive dossier I had put together—which included all the normal documentation as well as a form stating my blood type, some old airline tickets, and a greeting card from my accountant wishing me a prosperous new year—would be more than enough to establish my credentials. I was ready for anything, except what actually happened.

I had decided to support local industry and go to a dealer in Apt. The premises were not much bigger than an office, but they showed all the reassuring signs of efficiency. A computer hummed and hiccuped on the desk, the brochures were neatly arranged on racks, the aroma of freshly waxed coachwork was in the air, the place was spotless. Somehow, two cars had been squeezed into the small space, and they, too, were so highly polished that one hesitated to touch them. Here, I said to myself, was a dealer who meant business. The New Europe, even down in Provence.

But where *was* the dealer? After a few minutes I was beginning to feel lonely when a woman appeared from behind the rack of brochures and asked me what I wanted.

"I'd like to buy a car," I said.

"Ah. *Attends.*" She disappeared. Another few minutes went by. I started to read my third brochure, mesmerized by upholstery options and remote-control glove compartments, and barely glanced at a burly man in a checked shirt and flat cap who came in from the forecourt to join me by the rack.

"It is you who looks for a car," he said.

Indeed it was, I told him. I'd decided on the model, picked a color, chosen the upholstery. All that remained was to establish a price and a delivery date.

"*Ah bon.*" He tugged at his cap. "You need a salesman."

"I'm sorry. I thought that was you."

"*Beh non.* I take care of the forecourt. My son is the salesman."

"Then perhaps I could talk to your son."

"*Beh non.*" He shook his head. "He is *en vacances.*"

The gentleman in the cap could do nothing. But his son the salesman, so I was assured, would be back in a week or so, fit and rested. Meanwhile, as a special dispensation—brochures being the price they were these days, they didn't have many of them—I was allowed to keep the brochure so that I could study it at home.

It was either an admirable exercise in low-pressure salesmanship or a maddening inconvenience, depending on your patience and your point of view. Or, in my case, another reminder of why I like to live in Provence. Curiosities are everywhere, and the world's most reluctant car salesman is only one of them. Before leaving Apt, we should pay our respects to another—the town's railway station.

It is set back from the main road that leads to Avignon, a cream-colored building constructed during those giddy, prosperous days of the nineteenth century before trains had any real competition from cars and planes. The architectural style is railroad bourgeois—two substantial stories crowned by the triumphant, unblinking flourish of a circular *oeil-de-boeuf* window, its blank stare directed across the road toward the Hotel Victor Hugo directly opposite. (Rooms for the weary traveler at 175 francs a night, W.C. included.) To one side of the station building is a small, well-kept park, and the area in front is usually crowded with cars and vans coming and going. There is an air of bustle appropriate to the starting point for exotic voyages to every corner of Provence and beyond.

In fact, I wanted two seats on the TGV high-speed train from Avignon to Paris. Was it possible, I asked the gentleman at the reservations desk, to purchase tickets from him that would take us all the way?

"Of course," he said, pecking away at his computer to bring up the schedule of departures. "From here," he added proudly, "I can arrange tickets to anywhere in France—and also to London on the Eurostar, although that does involve changing trains at Lille. What time would be convenient for you to travel?"

I picked a time, and asked him when the train left from Apt to connect with the TGV from Avignon. He looked up from his computer with a frown, as though I had asked a question of extraordinary stupidity. "You can't go from *here*," he said.

"No?"

He stood up. *"Venez, monsieur."* I followed him to the back of the building, where he threw open a doorway that gave on to the deserted station platform and waved a hand at what had once been the track. I looked in vain for the shining double rails of the *chemin de fer,* for the signals, for the puff of steam on the horizon. Alas, there was no way for even the most determined train to penetrate the waist-high weeds that stretched in a straight line off into the distance. Apt's days as a vital rail link were clearly long gone. However, I was told that with sufficient notice a taxi to Avignon station could easily be arranged.

But think what you will about a train station without any trains, at least it is open all day to conduct its limited business. This sets it apart from those Provençal establishments—and there are many of them—which open and close according to a timetable that is guaranteed to bewilder and mystify the unwary. Butchers, *épiceries*, hardware stores, newsstands, antique dealers, clothes boutiques, and small stores of nearly every description seem to follow only one consistent rule: Whether they open at eight in the morning or not until ten, they lock their doors at lunchtime. The shutters come down at noon for at least two hours, often three. In small villages, this can stretch to four hours, particularly when the heat of summer calls for an extended siesta.

And just when you begin to feel that a certain chaotic pattern is emerging, the rules will change. You go to buy cheese at a shop that has always opened on the dot of three, only to find the window bare except for a notice advising you of a *fermeture exceptionelle*. Your first thought is that there has been a death in the family, but as the exceptional closing period enters its third week, you realize that a matter of almost equal gravity—the annual vacation—has come up. This is confirmed by Madame when she returns to work. Why didn't she put her holiday plans on the notice? Ah, because news of a prolonged absence might encourage burglars. Cheese theft, apparently, is a grim possibility in these dangerous times.

The rituals of rural commerce are made even more complicated every August, when the French by the millions leave their offices and factories for the joys of the open road and the peace of the countryside. Since Provence is a popular summer destination, most local enterprises keep working, hoping to profit from the high season. You will never have a problem finding food, drink, postcards, pottery, souvenirs made from olive wood, or suntan oil. But should you need anything a little out of the ordinary, something that originates in those deserted offices and factories up there in the far north, you would be well advised to anticipate a long wait.

Friends from Paris, down to spend August in their village house, discovered that their old electric kettle had expired. Being by nature faithful customers, they went back to the shop where they had bought it to buy a replacement. And there in the window, somewhat dusty but definitely new, was exactly what they wanted. They were already taking out their checkbook as they went into the shop.

The proprietor was apologetic, but firm. His stock of kettles was exhausted and, as the factory outside Paris was closed for the month, it would be mid-September before he received any more. *Désolé.*

But Monsieur, said our friends, you have a kettle—an up-to-date version of our old kettle, the very kettle we desire—in your window. What luck! We'll take that one.

The proprietor would have none of it. That kettle must remain in the window, he said, for reasons of publicity. How else would people know that I stock that particular *marque?*

Reasoned argument failed to budge him. The gift of the old kettle as substitute window dressing was declined. The offer of payment by cash, usually a powerful inducement, was refused. The kettle stayed in the shop window, where, for all I know, it is still gathering dust, a small token of the trials of August.

It is in many ways the most difficult month of the year, and not only because the population is swollen by tourists. Crowds can easily be avoided, but the weather can't, and the weather of August is, as the farmers say, *excessif,* a reaction to the heat that has built up during the long, dry days of July. For week after week, the sun never seems to set, soaking into the hills and the stone houses, melting tarmac, splitting earth, grilling the grass brown, thudding down to make the hair on your head hot to the touch. And then one day, traditionally around the middle of August, the air thickens and becomes heavy, almost syrupy. There is an abrupt silence in the bushes as the *cigales* stop chirping, and you feel that the countryside is holding its breath, waiting for the storm.

This still, quiet moment before the first trump of thunder is your final chance to go through the house unplugging your fax, your computer, your answering machine, your stereo, and your television set. Once the storm gets going and the lightning starts to ricochet around your ears, it is almost inevitable that the domestic power supply will be cut off. But before that happens there will often be one last violent electrical spasm—nature's vengeful swipe at high technology—powerful enough to scramble the brains of any sensitive appliance. We have lost two faxes in this way, and one answering machine that was so traumatized it developed an incurable stutter.

Our consolation is a front row seat for one of the greatest shows on earth. The valley acts like a monstrous amplifier for the rolling growls of thunder that swirl around the house, ending in cracks that threaten to shatter the roof tiles. Lightning dances along the crest of the mountains, and for a brilliant moment or two every rock and every tree is floodlit, their shapes etched against the evening sky. The dogs stay close to us, ears flat against their heads, content for once to be indoors. We eat by candlelight, grateful for the protection of solid stone walls, watching the storm move up the valley until it disappears with a distant mutter and a final flicker of light, far away in the hills of Haute Provence.

The air turns cool, then moist, as the first fat drops of

rain hit the ground, and there is the sudden welcome scent of wet earth. Within seconds, the drops become torrents. Water falls from the overhanging roof tiles in a continuous sheet, gouging channels in the gravel of the terrace, crushing plants, flooding flower beds, bouncing head-high off the outside table—two months' rain in half an hour. It stops as abruptly as it began, and we go paddling across the terrace to rescue a bedraggled parasol that has been knocked off its feet by the downpour.

The next morning the sky is as blue as ever and the sun returns, making steam rise from the newly washed fields. By the end of the day, the countryside has regained its parched appearance, as if the storm never happened. But inside the house, souvenirs of the deluge linger in the pipes and cisterns and U-shaped crannies of the plumbing system. Subterranean flooding causes prolonged gurgles. Normally mild-mannered faucets have violent sneezing attacks, spewing out gouts of muddy water. By some baffling process, items of kitchen waste—odd fragments of lettuce, a sprinkling of tea leaves—take a wrong turning in the pipes and find their way into the bowl of the downstairs lavatory, causing some consternation among visitors who are accustomed to uneventful urban plumbing. Well, they say, we never expected *this*.

But it is only one of many small surprises that make daily life in Provence unlike life anywhere else. One Sunday last summer, my wife came back from Coustellet market still shaking her head. She had been drawn to one of the stalls by a tray of *courgette* (squash) flowers, which are delicious either stuffed or deep-fried in light batter, a favorite late-summer recipe. I'd like half a kilo of those, she said.

But nothing is that simple. The stall-holder snapped off a plastic bag from a roll behind the stall. "Of course, Madame," he said. "Male or female?"

More recently, one of our guests, a man prone to the extravagant gesture while talking, knocked a glass of red wine over his trousers. The next day he took them to the dry cleaners. Madame spread the trousers on the counter, examining the stains with a professional eye and a discouraging shake of the head. It was possible, she said, that the stains could be removed, but that would depend on the wine. Was it a Châteauneuf or one of the lighter Luberon reds? Amazed that he couldn't remember, she then gave him a short lecture on the staining capabilities of various wines, according to their tannin content, and seemed ready to move on to particular vintages when the arrival of another customer distracted her.

Our friend returned to the house greatly impressed. He said he had spilled wine on his trousers all over Europe, and in several major cities in the United States. But never had the provenance of his stains been so thoroughly questioned. Next time this happened, he said, he would be sure to take the wine label and perhaps a few tasting notes in with his trousers.

The Provençal loves to give advice, to impart superior knowledge, to set you straight and save you from the error of your ways. As a foreigner who has had the temerity to write about Provence, I am frequently trapped in a corner with an accusing index finger wagging under my nose, and corrected. I've come to enjoy these educational exchanges, whether the subject is the best way to eat a melon or the mating habits of wild boars, and there have actually been occasions when conclusive evidence has been on my side. But this is dismissed or ignored. My instructor does not allow himself to be confused by the facts, and he will always have the last word.

One of the most persistent crimes that I have committed is to put an acute accent on the "e" in Luberon, an innocent but clearly uneducated act that inspires considerable scorn in the breast of the Provençal purist. Letters arrive, rapping me over the knuckles, quoting other writers such as Jean Giono and Henri Bosco, and telling me to follow their excellent, accentless examples. And then one day, Monsieur Farigoule, the self-anointed linguistics professor, took me to task for tinkering with someone else's language. In self-defense, I went back to my reference books.

It seemed to me that I had some rather distinguished and scholarly allies. In the Larousse dictionary, on the maps of the National Geographic Institute, in the *Etymological Dictionary of Names of Rivers and Mountains in France* and on the Michelin maps of the Vaucluse, the Luberon appears with an accent. These are not lightweight publications, but serious, official records, compiled by serious, official people. For once, I thought, the last word was going to be mine.

But no. As I recited the list to Farigoule, I could see him pursing his lips, and he allowed himself one or two eloquent, disdainful sniffs.

"Well," I said finally. "There you are. Larousse, Michelin . . ."

"*Bof,*" he said. "Parisians, all of them. What do they know?"

Ah, the poor Parisians. Despite being French they are regarded as foreign, and therefore to be treated with suspicion and ridicule. They are renowned for their arrogance, for their condescending attitude, for their fashionable clothes, for their shiny cars, for buying all the bread in the bakery, for just being Parisian. A derogatory word—*parisianisme*—is now creeping into the local language to describe their insidious and unwelcome influence on certain aspects of Provençal life, and they have even been accused of attempting to tamper with nature. Last year, a story circulated about the Parisian owners of summer homes in one of the more chic villages—*St. Germain sud,* as it has been called—complaining to the mayor about noise. Their siestas were being ruined, they claimed, by the insufferable racket of the *cigales.* How could anyone sleep with all these creatures rubbing their noisy legs together?

One might imagine the mayor treating this as a *crise municipale,* putting aside less important business to organize a squad of *cigale* hunters, armed with nets and insect sprays, to patrol the bushes on tiptoe, alert and ready to pounce on the merest whisper of a chirrup. It is more likely, of course, that the mayor gave the Parisians the standard Provençal response to unanswerable questions or ridiculous demands: the full shrug, which is executed by local experts as follows:

A certain amount of limbering-up is required before any major body parts are brought into action, and your first moves should be nothing more than a frown and a slight sideways tilt of the head. These indicate that you cannot believe the foolishness, the impertinence, or the plain dumb ignorance of what the Parisian has just said to you. There is a short period of silence before the Parisian tries again, repeating his remark and looking at you with some degree of irritation. Maybe he thinks you're deaf, or Belgian, and therefore confused by his sophisticated accent. Whatever he feels, you now have his complete attention.

This is the moment to demolish him and his nonsense with a flowing, unhurried series of movements as the full shrug is unfurled.

Step One. The jaw is pushed out as the mouth is turned down.
Step Two. The eyebrows are fully cocked and the head comes forward.
Step Three. The shoulders are raised to earlobe level, the elbows tucked in to the side, the hands fanning out with palms facing upward.
Step Four (optional). You allow a short, infinitely dismissive sound—something between flatulence and a sigh—to escape from your lips before letting the shoulders return to a resting position.

It might almost be a yoga exercise, and I must have seen it hundreds of times. It can be used to signify disagreement, disapproval, resignation, or contempt, and it effectively terminates any discussion. As far as I know, there is no countershrug, or satisfactory answering gesture. For these reasons, it is an invaluable gesture for anyone like myself whose command of the French language is far from perfect. A well-timed shrug speaks volumes.

I was on the receiving end of one not long ago when I went into Cavaillon, lured by reports of an elaborate facelift that had been given to the *toilettes publiques* at the top end of the Cours Bournissac. I remembered them as being unobtrusive and underground, dank in the winter and sweltering in summer; functional, certainly, and not a particular eyesore, but by no means decorative.

Changes have taken place, dramatic changes that are

obvious even from a distance. The top of the establishment has been covered by a circular bed of earth, planted
with bright flowers. In this floral setting, her face tilted
away from the sun, is a reclining nude carved from pale,
smooth stone. She undoubtedly has a symbolic significance, possibly something to do with rushing waters and
the joys of hygiene. In any event, she is a handsome and
well-formed addition to the Cavaillon landscape, promising blessed relief to those who venture down the stairs to
take advantage of the other improvements.

One of these is human, an attendant who will direct visitors to the appropriate section of the *toilettes* according to
gender and need in return for a modest tip. He is the first
surprise. The second is the choice of equipment. France
being a country that likes to embrace every kind of techno-
logical achievement from the Concorde to electronic mole
killers, you might expect to find a gleaming array of the
latest in sanitary engineering—automatically sterilized
cubicles at the very least, maybe with a seat-warmer
option for the colder months.

Instead, you will find a piece of bathroom history: a flat
porcelain tray about three feet square with a hole in the
middle and two rectangular protuberances, one on each
side of the hole, on which to place your feet. It is an
arrangement that has been in use since the earliest days of
modern plumbing, and is known in French sanitary circles
as the *à la turque* model. I had thought it was no longer
manufactured and virtually extinct, only to be found in
those corners of France that are too remote to benefit
from the march of progress. But there it was, solid, new,
and strangely out of place at the end of the twentieth
century.

Before leaving, I asked the attendant if he knew of any

reason why the contemporary lavatory had been passed over in favor of this more primitive installation. Was it to frustrate vandals? To discourage readers of magazines and others who might occupy the premises for selfishly long periods? An aesthetic choice? Or just nostalgia for the good old days? I might just as well have been asking him to explain the secret of life. He delivered the full shrug. "*C'est comme ça,*" he said. That's how it is. Take it or leave it.

What is there to like about this catalogue of Provençal quirks, most of which are inconvenient and seem to have been devised with the express purpose of taking up as much of your time as possible? An errand that might take half an hour in other, more streamlined societies can easily occupy an entire morning. Appointments are postponed or forgotten. The simplest domestic problems always seem to require complicated solutions. Very little is straightforward. The climate is intemperate, often destructive. And the foreign resident, whether Parisian, Dutch, German, or British, no matter how many years he may spend in Provence, will never be considered anything more than a long-term tourist. These are not conventional attractions.

And yet I like them, almost all of them, almost all the time. They are part of the character of the place and of the people. It's true that a number of accommodations have been made for visitors—there are more festivals, more small hotels, more restaurants, an increased willingness to accept new technology. It's not unusual, for example, to see cell phones glued to the dusty ears of tractor drivers in the vineyards, and sometimes I have the feeling that Provence is attempting to do the splits, with one foot in the past and the other testing the temperature of the future. But I don't see much in the way of fundamental change since the first time I came here more than twenty years ago.

Life has not accelerated, but still dawdles along keeping time with the seasons. The markets still sell real food that has escaped the modern passion for sterilizing and shrink-wrapping. The countryside is still wild, and unscarred by golf courses, theme parks, or condominium colonies. It is still possible to listen to silence. Unlike so many other beautiful parts of the world which progress and ease of access have made noisy, predictable, and bland, Provence has managed to retain its individual flavor and personality. This can be delightful or exasperating, like a difficult, cantankerous old friend. But that's the way it is, with no excuses. Take it or leave it.

A Beginner's Guide
to Marseille

Besides Paris, I can think of only one other city in France with a distinct, internationally known personality. Mention Lille or Lyon, St.-Etienne or Clermont-Ferrand, and you are unlikely to encounter too many strongly held opinions. Mention Marseille, and practically everyone will have a clear, if often uninformed, idea of the character of the place.

Alas, it is not likely to be wholesome. Drunken sailors brawling on the Canebière; louche behavior in the dockside bars; the grim, ancient prison of the Château d'If; narrow backstreets where the visitor ventures at his peril after dark; and, thanks to *The French Connection*, a suspicion that not only fish are changing hands at the daily market on the Quai des Belges. Marseille is generally seen as raffish, exotic, and more than a little dangerous. It's a view that is not necessarily confined to foreigners. I remember being warned about the city many years ago by my neighbor Faustin. He had only been there once in his life, and he had no plans to repeat the experience. I asked what had happened to him, and he just shook his head. But he told me that if he ever had to go back he would take his gun.

And yet there is no place that could have had a more romantic beginning. According to legend—kept alive and embellished, no doubt, by the Marseillais' liking for a good story—the city was founded on love. Five hundred and ninety-nine years before Christ, a Phocaean navigator named Protis hit the beach just in time for a nuptial banquet given by the local king, whose name was Nann. In the course of the banquet, the king's daughter, Gyptis, took one look at the young navigator and decided that he was the one for her. It was a lightning bolt, a *coup de foudre,* and as a wedding gift the king presented the happy couple with a hundred and fifty acres of prime seafront property on which to set up house. Thus Marseille was born. It has been continuously inhabited ever since, for twenty-six centuries, and the population has expanded from two to around a million.

Like the city, the inhabitants have a reputation that is, as their critics say, *un peu spécial*—special, in this case, not being the complimentary label it usually is in English. The Marseillais is suspected of stretching the truth from time to time, of embroidering and exaggerating. I wonder if this is because Marseille is a fish town, and the environment somehow encourages the natural instinct of the fisherman to improve on nature. Only in the sea around Marseille, so the story goes, do sardines regularly grow to the size of young sharks. Should you ask to see one of these marvels, you will be told it's the wrong time of the month; the moon must be full. Or, if the moon happens to be full when you ask, you will be told to be patient. It is only at the time of the new moon when the giant sardine can be observed. To be fair, this advice is usually delivered with a nudge and a wink, and you are not really expected to take it seriously. Nevertheless, the reputation exists. I was told that you should take several grains of salt whenever you go to Marseille, and to use them frequently in the course of conversation.

That is, of course, if you can understand what is being said. Marseille has never been happy with the idea of being told what to do by a central government, and there is a long history of rebellion against officials in Paris, even down to the pomposities of their speech. Consequently, Marseille does its best to avoid speaking official French. This is partly achieved by the accent, and there is a kind of shagginess about the pronunciation which can make even familiar words sound as though they have been marinated in some thick linguistic sauce. When this is applied to the unfamiliar words and conversational quirks that are peculiar to Marseille, you find yourself wondering if you've been tossed into the swirling currents of a new language.

Here is just one of the many phrases that defeated me until I asked for it to be written down: *"L'avillon, c'est plus rapide que le camillon, même si y a pas de peuneus."* The plane is faster than the truck, even if there aren't any tires. A simple enough sentence in French, but garnished with the Marseille marinade it becomes incomprehensible. Imagine the difficulties when the phrase being spoken is a local invention, such as: "*Il est un vrai cul cousu.*" The polite translation for this is a man who is lacking in a sense of humor, and who very rarely smiles. Or, more literally, a man who has his backside sewn up. If, in addition to his morose disposition, the poor fellow is thought to be seriously deranged, then "*Il est bon pour le cinquante-quatre,*" a reference to the number 54 tram which stopped at the hospital that used to treat mental disorders.

Not even the names lovingly chosen by parents for their offspring can escape the Marseille treatment. André, whether he likes it or not, becomes *Dédou,* Francis becomes *Sissou,* Louise becomes *Zize.* As they grow up, the children will learn to use words that one is unlikely to hear anywhere else in France: words like *momo* and *mafalou, toti* and *scoumougne* and *cafoutchi.* It is a language within a language, sometimes very close to the old Provençal dialects, sometimes borrowing from the immigrants who have come to Marseille over the centuries from Italy, Algeria, Greece, Armenia, and heaven knows where else. A stew of speech, rich and often ripe, guaranteed to bewilder the newly arrived visitor.

But the first obstacle to be overcome is finding the center of town. The most direct and spectacular way to arrive is by sea, a route that would probably find you agreeing with Madame de Sévigné, who was "overwhelmed by the singular beauty of this town." From a boat, you would see it all: the neat rectangular form of the old port, the sprawl of the city, and, high above, the glint of gold from the statue of Notre Dame de la Garde. But if you arrive by road, as we did, your first impressions will be somewhat lacking in singular beauty. The outskirts of modern Marseille are not what Madame de Sévigné had in mind; they are dreary. Traffic is on several levels, darting in and out of tunnels and along overpasses through the kind of architecture that makes you want to take up demolition as a hobby.

Eventually, more by luck than a command of local geography, we managed to find our way to the old port, and the scenery took an instant turn for the better. There is always a magic about arriving in a city on the sea—the sudden unfolding of a long view to the horizon after congested streets, the change in the air from fumes to fresh brine, and, in Marseille, the hubbub of the fish-sellers drumming up trade.

They are there on the eastern side of the port from about eight o'clock each morning, rubber booted and leather faced, standing and shouting behind shallow boxes the size of small dining tables. The catch of the day, often still alive and kicking, shimmers in the sun, silver and gray and blue and red, the odd reproachful eye looking up at you as you walk by. Pause for a second, and Madame—it seems that the husbands do the catching and their wives do the selling—plucks a fish from her tray and holds it under your nose. "Here," she says, "smell the sea!" She gives the fish an appreciative slap, and it twitches. "I must be mad," she says, "I'm selling a live one for the price of a dead one! Fish is good for your brain, fish is good for your love life, *venez, la mamie, venez!*" The customers look and sniff and buy, walking off with their blue plastic bags, the contents still flapping, held carefully away from their bodies.

In the harbor behind the stalls, the water is covered with a bobbing mosaic of boats, so closely moored that you feel you could walk several hundred yards out to sea without getting your feet wet. Floating gin palaces, day sailers, graceful yachts with the sheen of a dozen coats of varnish, and the fat-bellied ferries that will take you across the mile or so that separates the mainland from the bleak little island with the sinister reputation.

The Château d'If, an earlier version of Alcatraz, was built in the sixteenth century, and was used to keep undesirables at a safe distance from the city. A small consolation for the inmates was the clean sea air; a daily torment must have been the sight of Marseille—a picturesque view of liberty—across the water. It is a setting that could have been devised in a novel, and so it's not surprising to learn that the Château d'If's most famous prisoner, the Count of Monte Cristo, never existed. Alexandre Dumas *père* invented him, and lived to see his invention commemorated when the authorities, not wanting to disappoint Dumas's readers, provided an official Count of Monte Cristo cell. But there was no shortage of genuine prisoners. At one time, thousands of Protestants were kept here before going on to become galley slaves. And, an example of the law being as absurd then as it often is today, there was the unfortunate Monsieur de Niozelles, who committed the unspeakable crime of failing to remove his hat in front of the king. Shock and horror ensued, followed by a sentence of six years in solitary confinement on the island. No wonder royalty came to a sticky end in France.

A short sea voyage, we thought, would be a bracing way to start the day, and we went to the quayside office to buy tickets for the ferry. The young man at the counter barely raised his head. "Not this morning," he said. "The weather."

The weather was ideal, sunny and mild. The ferry, which we could see behind him, looked substantial enough to cross the Atlantic, let alone the sheet of glass that stretched between us and the Château d'If. What was the problem with the weather? we asked.

"The mistral."

There was a hesitant breeze, no more. Certainly nothing that would qualify as a life-threatening storm. "But there isn't a mistral."

"There will be."

"Then why are you here?"

That provoked the first shrug of the day, against which there is no argument. Leaving the quay, we were stopped by a small, dark man who wagged an agitated finger at my wife. "Put it away," he told her, pointing at the camera slung from her shoulder. "Put it in your bag. This is Marseille."

We looked around for gangs of camera thieves, sailors out of control on shore leave, dark-windowed cars carrying senior executives from the underworld, or indeed any sign of menace. There was none. The sun was warm, the cafés were full, the sidewalks busy in that slow-moving way you find in Mediterranean towns, where nobody seems to be in a hurry to go anywhere. The Marseille version of the man in the street, we noticed, is often more prosperously padded than his counterpart in the country, and we saw more impressive stomachs in half an hour than we normally see in a week. And the human color scheme is different, many of the faces reflecting the various tints of Africa, from café au lait to the deep gleaming black of Senegal.

We turned up the Canebière, the broad boulevard leading east from the port. Once a southern Champs-Elysées, this has now gone the way of many grand avenues around the world, and unless you have a particular interest in the offices of banks, airlines, and travel agents, there isn't much to detain you. However, keep walking and turn left on to the Boulevard Dugommier, and you'll eventually come to one of the sights on everyone's list, the Saint-Charles station. Or rather, the staircase leading down from the station—a wide, nineteenth-century folly of a staircase, a film set of a staircase, decorated with statues representing Asia and Africa, the perfect spot to make your grand entrance to Marseille as long as you don't have heavy suitcases. And from here, if time or aching feet have become a problem, you can duck underground and try the Marseille metro.

My record with underground transit systems is one of almost unbroken failure. I can, and do, get lost in the bowels of London, New York, or Paris as quickly as most people buy a ticket. But the Marseille system, even to someone who has a useless void where his sense of direction ought to be, is delightfully compact and straightforward. Fifteen minutes after leaving the station, we were on the south side of the Vieux Port, walking along the Corniche in the general direction of lunch.

It was one of the most pleasant strolls I have ever had in a city. Above the modern skyline, there were occasional golden glimpses of Notre Dame de la Gare. The sea was just below us, the views across to the Frioul islands were glorious, the air was balmy. On the sloping ledges of rock between the road and the sea, figures were stretched out taking the Indian summer sunshine. One man, who appeared to be totally naked except for a rubber bathing hat, was swimming, jerking forward with froglike kicks, his body pale against the dark blue water. It was more like June than October.

The coastline here has been nibbled into a succession of tiny coves, or *anses*, not all of them with reassuring

names. The Anse de Maldormé conjures up a colony
of insomniacs, with their neighbors the counterfeiters
installed not far away in the Anse de la Fausse Monnaie.
Our destination was the Anse des Auffes (highly respectable ropemakers), home of a long-established restaurant with the engaging name of Chez Fonfon. There, we
had been told, one could eat fish so fresh they winked at
you as they came to the table.

Coming down from the Corniche into the Anse des
Auffes, we felt we had left the city to find ourselves in a
miniature fishing village. Boats were pulled up to a small
ramp. Two children played football among the tables and
chairs of a restaurant terrace. An optimist with an attaché
case at his feet stood on the quay with his fishing rod, the
line dangling in a slick of shallow water that was iridescent
with diesel oil. It was washday, and the local laundry was
festooned across the facades of the houses—a bunting of
underwear, brilliant reds, purples, and greens interspersed
with the more sober and matronly dark peach. Why is it
that washing lines are more colorful in the south than in
the white and pastel north? Is lingerie, like so much else,
influenced by climate? It would be hard to imagine coming across such a vibrant and extrovert display in Man-
chester or Scarsdale.

After the dazzle of the underwear, the interior of Chez
Fonfon seemed muted and unremarkable; a pleasant, sen-
sible room with no visible efforts at an obvious style. The
clients, in any case, were far too busy with the menus to
notice decorative refinements. They were here for the fish.

If you ever speak of Marseille and fish in the same
breath—at least in southern France—be warned. There
will be a *bouillabaisse* expert close by, and he or she will
not rest until you have been persuaded of the merits and

the undoubted superiority of one particular recipe over another. There is an official guarantee of the correct ingredients, the *Charte de la Bouillabaisse*, which you will see displayed outside serious restaurants all over Marseille. But should you go a few miles down the coast to Toulon, your charter from Marseille will be treated with no more respect than a parking ticket. The problem is the potato.

In Toulon, *bouillabaisse* isn't *bouillabaisse* without potatoes; in Marseille it would be sacrilege to include potatoes. There is a similar difference of opinion over lobster. Is it in or is it out? It depends where you go. One of these days, all disputes will be settled by the Commission of Human Rights in Brussels, or the Michelin guide, or the Minister of the Interior (whose responsibilities surely include the stomach) in Paris. Until then, the closest we can get to a noncontroversial *bouillabaisse* is one that embraces the following basic methods and ingredients:

First and most important, the fish must be fresh and they must come only from the Mediterranean. (Restaurants in Tokyo, New York, and London that promise *bouillabaisse* on their menus are fibbing.) The types of fish can vary, but there is one essential: the *rascasse*, a creature of truly horrible appearance with a face that only a mother could love, traditionally cooked and served with the hideous head still attached. This is not to give you a nightmare, but to let you extract the flesh of the cheeks, supposedly the tastiest parts. The rest of the *rascasse* is fairly bland, but experts say it somehow brings out the flavor in its companions as they are cooked together on a low boil in a saffron and garlic flavored soup.

The soup and fish come to the table separately, the soup with slices of toast, the fish with *rouille*, a high-voltage, rust-colored paste made with oil, chili peppers, and yet more garlic. The immediate result is delicious, a pungent mixture of spices and the sea. The longer-term effects of such heroic doses of garlic are undoubtedly antisocial, and we were confident we'd be safe that afternoon from the attentions of any back-alley mugger; one well-directed breath from us, and he'd shrivel, or run a mile.

The back alleys we had decided to explore were those of Le Panier, the oldest quarter in Marseille. A large part of it—home to twenty thousand people—was blown up in World War II by the Nazis when they realized that it was a haven for Jewish refugees and members of the Resistance. What remains is a tangle of steep, narrow streets, some of them paved in a decidedly nonchalant manner, some stepped, and lined on either side with houses of a picturesque seediness. Cars are rare; we saw only two. The first came nosing out of a side alley like a lost dog; its driver saw that it was too narrow to turn either left or right, and had to retreat backwards. The second car stays in my memory because of an impossible feat of parking.

We were passing an extremely thin house, only as wide as a single room, and glanced through the open door. One side of the room was furnished normally, with carpet, table, and chairs. Three members of the family were sitting there watching television. The other half of the room was taken up by a well-polished Citroën. It wasn't one of the bigger Citroëns, admittedly, but big enough, and somehow it had managed to creep in through the door and park itself without obliterating the furniture. I wondered how long it had been there, and if it was ever allowed out for a run.

Presumably, it had been confined to the living room to keep it safe in what we had been told was an unsafe neighborhood. But once again, Marseille was failing to live down to its reputation. Children and old ladies were out in force, not visibly in terror of their lives. Many of the houses had their doors and windows wide open, and one or two had been turned into tiny restaurants and *épiceries*. It was more charming than threatening, the only risk of physical injury coming from the occasional flying soccer ball.

As we reached the top end of the Rue du Petit-Puits, we had our first sight of one of Marseille's most fortunate and elegant survivors, the pale, rosy stone mass of La Vieille Charité. Designed by Pierre Puget and built in the seventeenth and eighteenth centuries, the buildings at one time provided a home for Marseille's homeless, who were probably too relieved at finding shelter to appreciate that they had been installed in some kind of architectural heaven: a vast quadrangle, nearly a hundred yards long by fifty yards wide, surrounded by three stories of arcades which overlook a magnificent chapel topped by an oval dome.

In fact, despite its name, its early history is far from charitable. The residents of seventeenth-century Marseille—or at least those with a roof over their heads and money in their pockets—were alarmed at the number of beggars and vagabonds roaming the streets, who were considered a source of unrest and delinquency. Clearly, the city needed its own squad of riot police, and so a sergeant and ten archers dressed in red were hired to round up and imprison all those without resources who couldn't prove they were natives of Marseille. These duties were performed with such enthusiasm that in 1695 twelve hundred men and women were crammed into La Charité. They were put to work under the direction of armed supervisors, but were allowed out from time to time, closely guarded, to make up the numbers in funeral processions.

Came the Revolution, and La Charité became more charitable. Over the centuries, it offered shelter to a long, sad list of temporary tenants: the elderly, the destitute, and the orphans, the families displaced by urban redevelopment, and finally, those evicted by Nazi dynamite. And then, the war over, it was left to rot.

It took more than twenty years of enlightened restoration to bring it up to its present immaculate state. Perhaps because we had arrived through cramped and shadowy streets, the impression of space and light as we stood in the quadrangle was almost overpowering. It was a moment for looking rather than talking. There is something about architecture on the grand scale that tends to subdue human speech, and the thirty or forty people wandering around the arcades never raised their voices above a murmur. Not quite an awed hush, but very close. As it happened, we were told that we had picked a quiet day, a between-season lull in the program of events and exhibitions. Even so, there is a museum of Mediterranean Archeology and an excellent bookshop on the premises, and these can easily take up the rest of your afternoon.

We walked back to the port and a more recent local monument, Le New-York, a brasserie with a west-facing terrace and a view of the spectacular Marseille sunset. The day had been too short, and there was too much we hadn't seen: the Château d'If, due to the weather (which remained perfect throughout the day); the many museums; the dozens of fine old buildings hidden among the high-rises; the cathedrals (one of them supported by 444 marble columns); the Bar de la Marine, where the characters in Pagnol's *Marius* played cards; the Château du

Pharo, built by Napoléon III for his wife; and Marseille's stomach, the Marché des Capucins.

But although a day in a city is no more than a sip from a barrel, it had been enough to make us want to come back for more. Marseille may be a rough old girl with a dubious reputation, but she has considerable charm, and there are patches of great beauty among the modern ugliness. Also, I happen to like Marseille's independent, slightly overblown personality, and I particularly admire the cheek with which it has appropriated both the French national anthem and the most popular aperitif in Provence.

"La Marseillaise," that stirring call to children of the motherland, was actually composed in Strasbourg as the battle song of the army of the Rhine. It was taken up and sung by five hundred volunteers from Marseille who were marching to Paris, and when they reached the capital it became, of course, *"la chanson marseillaise"* that they were singing. (In fairness, it does sound a great deal better than "La Strasbourgeoise" as the title of France's number one song.)

More recently, Paul Ricard, who became Marseille's most celebrated and flamboyant tycoon—he once took fifteen hundred of his staff to Rome to be blessed by the Pope—decided as a young man to make his own brand of pastis. It wasn't an original idea. The Pernod distillery near Avignon had turned its production over to pastis when the dangerously addictive absinthe was banned in 1915. But Pernod didn't invent pastis either; according to legend, a hermit did. As you would expect from an ambitious, gregarious hermit, he took his invention and opened a bar—in Marseille, naturally. But it was Ricard, with his genius for publicity and marketing, who gave the drink its Mediterranean pedigree. He, and he alone, made what he called *le vrai pastis de Marseille.* He promoted the phrase as if it were a guarantee of the genuine article. And it worked. Something over fifty million bottles a year are sold now.

A final story that illustrates Marseille's independence of spirit: After years of cocking a snook at central authority, which in those days was Louis XIV, the city was taught a lesson. The walls were breached and the cannons of the fort protecting Marseille from attack by sea were turned around and aimed at the inhabitants, who were considered more of a threat than any invaders.

I don't know exactly why, but it gives me pleasure to think that the Marseillais are still here, as rebellious as ever, while the kings are long since gone.

How to Be a Nose

Drive north from Apt, and within an hour you will be in Haute Provence. This was the setting for Jean Giono's novels, and a place he sometimes saw with a dark and unforgiving eye. Here is one of his less inviting descriptions: "The houses are half caved in. In the streets overgrown with nettles, the wind roars, bellows, bawls out its music through the holes of shutterless windows and open doors."

It might be that in the interests of literature he was taking an extreme view, but it's one that reflects the nature of the place—wild, empty, and hard. Coming from the cultivated prettiness of the Luberon, with its postcard villages, carefully restored houses, cherry orchards, and row after orderly row of vines, Haute Provence feels like another world, great stretches of it deserted and virtually untouched. Villages are separated by miles of countryside, sometimes jagged and bleak, sometimes rolling and beautiful. The sky is vast. If you stop your car to listen to the scenery, you might hear the distant, hollow clank of goat bells coming from an invisible herd. Otherwise, there is the wind.

Drive on, past l'Observatoire de Haute Provence, where they say you can breathe the clearest, purest air in France, and head for the foothills of the Montagne de Lure. There, set in a bowl of lavender fields, you will find Lardiers, a village of perhaps a hundred inhabitants. Their houses are bunched around the Mairie and the Café de la Lavande—the kind of restaurant one always hopes to find at the end of a day's drive: good food, good wine, and charm in equal doses.

Lardiers is an unlikely place to find a journalist, let alone dozens of them. But on a sunny day in June, with the lavender just turning from gray-green to purple, the press had turned out in force and come to the village for the opening of an educational institution which, as far as I know, is unique.

The idea started in Manosque, Giono's hometown and the headquarters of one of the few genuinely Provençal companies to have an international reputation. L'Occitane made its name by word of nose. Its soaps, its oils and essences, its shampoos and creams, are made in Provence, many of them with ingredients grown in the local fields. Not only the lavender that you would expect, but sage, rosemary, fresh herbs, honey, peaches, and almonds.

Depending on your inclination, you can have a peach-scented bath, a rubdown with oil of thyme, or a shave that tingles with rosemary. And not long ago another ingredient was introduced, simple and obvious in hindsight, as many good ideas are: Labels were printed in two languages, the second being Braille. This made it possible for the contents of a jar or a bottle on the bathroom shelf to be read by the fingertips as well as by the eye. From here, another idea evolved, based on the adjustments that nature makes to the human body when one of its primary functions is affected—in this case, the ability to see.

To make up in some way for the loss of sight, the other senses compensate by becoming more acute, particularly the sense of smell. A company whose business is fragrance is always interested in finding sensitive and educated noses. Perfumes are never accidents, but recipes, usually very complex recipes—a balance between sweet and sharp, a cocktail of essences. Choosing, mixing, and judging these is a great art, and great artists are as rare in the perfume world as they are anywhere else. For a start, they need to be born with a natural aptitude for the work, and the most important requirement is an unusually receptive nose—a nose in a million. Over the years, with the proper training, this can be developed until it is capable of identifying even the ghost of a fragrance—the crucial drop that lifts a perfume from the ordinary to the unforgettable. But first, you have to find those talented nostrils.

Where does one look? It's relatively easy to spot outstanding ability in almost everything from football to mathematics, from music to languages. These are gifts that become evident quite early. A hypersensitive nose, though, is a hidden asset—personal, private, and, under normal circumstances, not likely to be noticed. Imagine two mothers comparing the merits of their children, for instance. "Well, I know Jean-Paul's a mischievous little brute, and it's true I caught him biting his sister on the leg the other day—but I can forgive him everything because he has such a wonderful sense of smell." It doesn't happen. The young nose is a neglected organ.

This is something the people at L'Occitane started to change on that sunny day in June, when a handful of pupils arrived in Lardiers for the opening session of a different kind of school. The pupils were between the ages of ten and seventeen, and they were blind.

The official name of this academy of the nose is *L'Ecole d'Initiation aux Arts et aux Métiers du Parfum destinées aux Enfants Aveugles* (The School of Initiation to the Arts and Skills of Perfumery for Blind Children). The classroom is in a small stone building on the edge of the village, and it will probably never again see so many international visitors. The journalists had come from North America, Europe, Hong Kong, Australia, and Japan, noses and notebooks at the ready as the pupils took their places around a long table in the center of the room.

Classroom equipment was laid out in front of each pupil: flasks of different fragrances and a supply of paper tapers. Lesson one was the technique of the informed sniff, and I quickly learned where I had been going wrong all these years. My instinct when presented with something to smell has always been to take aim with my nose and breathe in like a drowning man coming up for the third time. This method, so I was tactfully informed, is recommended for sinus sufferers inhaling medication; any fragrance student caught behaving like that would go straight to the bottom of the class. Apparently, prolonged nasal suction—I think that was the technical term—delivers a knockout blow to delicate membranes, making further olfactory investigation temporarily impossible.

Having failed the first test, I was taken aside and shown how sniffing—or, more elegantly, "tasting with the nose"—should be done. The demonstration looked marvelously graceful, like an orchestra conductor limbering up with his baton before attacking the woodwind section. The end of a taper was dipped into the fragrance to absorb a few drops, then removed and passed beneath the nostrils in a single flowing motion that ended with a jaunty upward flick of the hand. This brief moment is enough for the nose to register the aroma. A message is sent to the brain for reaction and analysis. *Et voilà.* There is no need, I was told again, for crude and prolonged snorting.

Watching the pupils, it was clear that they were doing a great deal better than I had done with the technique of the sniff, and it was wonderful to see the mixture of furious concentration and pleased surprise on their faces as they began to read the signals picked up by their noses.

To help them, they had a formidable professor, Lucien Ferrero, who must have one of the most experienced and knowledgeable noses in France, and who has personally created more than two thousand perfumes. He had come from Grasse to take the class through its paces, to train young noses in good habits, and, with a little luck, to discover talent that could be developed.

Ferrero is one of life's natural teachers. He has a passion for his subject and, unlike many experts, the ability to explain it with clarity and a sense of humor. The children could understand him—even I could understand him—as he described how perfume works on two levels, the perception by the nose and the interpretation by the brain; and the five broad types of perfume, from alcoholic to the *couverture des mauvaises odeurs.* (This accompanied by giggles from the class and a most eloquent wrinkling of the professorial nostrils.)

The first session was no longer than an hour or so, partly because of one of the hazards of the occupation: the onset of *fatigue nasale.* After a while, even the most eager and professional noses become tired and lose their ability to concentrate. But also, this being France and the hour being close to noon, it was necessary to put academic matters aside for lunch. Long tables had been set up on the terrace outside the classroom, the Café de la Lavande had provided the menu, and I sat down with more journalists than I'd ever seen in one place.

It was a slightly uncomfortable moment. My previous experience with the press en masse had been several years ago, during our time in Ménerbes, when it seemed that every British newspaper was going through a period of discovering Provence. Reporters would turn up on the doorstep, bristling with questions, their tape machines cocked to record the slightest indiscretion. If, as usually happened, I couldn't give them much of a story, they would ambush my neighbor Faustin on his tractor in the vineyard and interview him. Photographers flitted around in the bushes. One eager little news editor sent a fax to my wife expressing his great sorrow at our impending divorce (fortunately, she's still putting up with me), and asking if, as he phrased it, she would care to share her private feelings with his two million readers. Another paper printed a map showing where our house could be found; yet another printed our telephone number. In both cases, the information was wildly inaccurate, and someone else must have had the pleasure of unexpected visits and calls from British strangers. The final accolade was a letter from a tabloid offering to buy the house so that it could be given away as a prize in a sweepstakes to boost circulation. Exciting days indeed.

It was with some relief that I found myself sitting among reporters who were more interested in the school than in our domestic arrangements. They were mostly health editors and beauty editors, experts in skin care, makeup, and the correct way to pluck eyebrows, students of cellulite and disciples of the balanced diet. Would these ethereal creatures, I wondered, be able to hold their own with the Provençal version of a light summer meal? There were three copious courses, including a sturdy *aioli* with cod and potatoes, and enough wine to sink the afternoon without trace.

From previous experience with the press, I should have known that professional training would come to the rescue. Journalists differ in their areas of interest, in their writing styles, in their aptitude for research, and their ability to dig out a story. Some have prodigious memories, others rely on tape or shorthand. But in one respect they are alike: All journalists are good at lunch, and these women could pack it away with the best of them. When I looked down the table as coffee was served, the only bottles I could see with any remaining moisture were those containing mineral water.

National characteristics then began to emerge. Anglo-Saxons tended to sit back and take their ease, giving in to a drowsy, after-lunch languor. But the journalists from the Far East, showing astonishing vigor, jumped up, unsheathed their Nikons, and clicked away at the view. I thought it a great pity that cameras can't record what noses can, because the scent of a fine hot day in Haute Provence is every bit as evocative as the sight of lavender and sage fields disappearing into the glare of the sun. Baked earth and rocks, the tartness of herbs, the warmth of the breeze, the smell of spiced heat—it's a distillation of the scenery. No doubt one day they'll put it in a bottle.

Meanwhile, a fragrant afternoon had been organized, with the first stop a demonstration of another kind of cookery. A few miles away, at the Rocher d'Ongles, plants were being turned into oil. I think I was expecting men in white coats pressing buttons in a laboratory; what I found was a huge, open-sided shed vibrating with heat, its tall chimney sending out clouds of scented smoke. It looked as though Rube Goldberg had been in charge of construction, and the head alchemist, far from being a white-coated technician, was dressed in a very unscientific T-shirt and canvas trousers. But he could certainly cook.

It's a recipe that uses the most basic ingredients: plants, fire, and water. At one end of a contorted arrangement of tubes, pipes, and vats, water is heated, and the steam produced passes through a tube to the plants—in this case, what looked like half a ton of rosemary. Steam releases the plant's volatile elements, carrying them through to a coil, and from there to a condenser circulating cold water. The steam then liquefies, and the essential oil rises to the top of the water. Scoop this off, put it in a flask, and there you have five-star V.S.O.P. essence of rosemary. The same process is used with rose, lemon, mint, geranium, thyme, pine, eucalyptus, and dozens of other plants and flowers.

Looking around, I was struck by the contrast between the place of origination and the eventual place of use. Here we were in a primitive building in the middle of a field, sweating like prisoners in a sauna, watching great clumps of vegetation being boiled in equipment that resembled a giant chemistry set for beginners. And where was it all going to end? About as far from its modest beginnings as you can imagine—on a dressing table or a shelf in some perfumed enclave, dabbed on drop by drop.

Moist, but more knowledgeable, we left the furnace heat of the distillery for the priory of Salagon, built in the twelfth century for Benedictine monks, abandoned during the Revolution, and now restored as the home of the Heritage Conservatory of Haute Provence.

It is always amazing to me that buildings like this, with their massive blocks of stone and great, perfectly formed spans of vaulting, could have been constructed without the aid of modern machinery. No cranes, no hydraulic winches, no electrically powered stonecutters—just hand and eye and an infinite amount of back-breaking labor. I couldn't help thinking of the months it took us to restore a small house, and I took my hat off to the extraordinary patience of those monks of eight hundred years ago.

They would have approved of a recent addition to the church grounds, which was what we had come to see: a large botanical garden, laid out in that meticulously ordered way the French adopt when they want to show nature who's in charge. No irregularities, no wayward and undisciplined twigs, none of nature's summer abandon. The plants, in their perfect little squares, were organized by scent as well as by species, and we were given a conducted tour, sniffing as we went, through carpets of green, gray, and blue. Everything had its Latin tag, and there was not a weed to be seen. I had the feeling that lizards would be treated as trespassers.

By now, the sun was beginning to dip, and many of us were doing the same. After a long, hot afternoon, *fatigue nasale* had set in, and we could sniff no more. It was time to give the senses a rest before the final event of the day.

Dinner was outside, at half a dozen long tables in the garden of an old farm in the hills above the village of Mane, and the aperitifs were having a rejuvenating effect on the press corps. It was, so one beauty editor told me, a considerable improvement over her last assignment, which had involved slime baths and a diet of lettuce and lemon juice at a health spa. She was a woman who admitted to having a demanding appetite, and claimed that she found it impossible to write on an empty stomach. She loved being sent on a job where the rations were good. France, for her, was food.

This made me wonder how the others were reacting to their first taste of Provence, and when I asked them it was interesting to find an almost total lack of consistency. The Japanese couldn't get over the size of the houses, the enormous tracts of empty land, the absence of crowds, noise, and high-rise buildings. They found the food "interesting" and the wine strong, but what really impressed them was the luxury of space—almost inconceivable to someone sentenced to life in a Tokyo apartment.

The Americans were accustomed to space, and even some of the countryside of Haute Provence looked vaguely familiar; not unlike the Napa Valley without cars, as one woman said. Her initial impressions were the crumbling beauty of the buildings—"they're so *old*"—and, not surprisingly from someone coming from the world capital of efficient hygiene, the incomprehensible mysteries of French plumbing. How do they take a shower, she wondered, when you have to hold the shower head with one hand and the soap with the other? Or do they do it in pairs?

The British, fresh from a typical early summer at home—scattered showers developing later into rain—loved the light, the heat, and the chance to eat outdoors. One woman, casting a professional beauty-editor's eye over my face and trying to suppress a wince, said that too much sun is very aging. But on the whole, the journalists approved of the climate, and they were also pleased to discover that the people in Provence were actually "quite nice, and not at all *snotty,* like the Parisians are." The poor Parisians, everyone's favorite target.

It was a good evening, and it had been a good day. No new school could have hoped for more attention at the beginning of its first term, and for once nobody was there to criticize. We all wanted the idea to succeed.

Partly to find out if it had, and partly to continue the education of my own nose, we went some months later to see Lucien Ferrero again, this time at his office outside Grasse. I'd never been to Grasse; all I knew was that it had been the center of the perfume industry in France since the early nineteenth century. I had visions of old men in straw hats pushing wheelbarrows piled with rose petals, of rickety tin-roofed distilleries like the one at Rocher d'Ongles, of entire streets and most of the population smelling of mimosa or Chanel No. 5. These fancies faded in a traffic jam going into town, and disappeared altogether at the sight of reality. Grasse was busy, crowded, and workmanlike.

It fell into the perfume business through a combination of luck, sheep, buffalo, and Catherine de Médici. In the Middle Ages, Grasse was a tanning town, treating sheepskins from Provence and buffalo hides from Italy. Part of the process required the use of aromatic herbs (and if you've ever smelt a tannery, you'll understand why). And then fashion came along to set the town off in a new direction.

There was an outbreak of elegance in Renaissance Italy. Perfumed gloves became all the rage, and anyone with an eye for the essentials of life insisted on having fragrant, well-dressed fingers. Catherine de Médici, in her capacity as fashion consultant to the aristocracy, arranged for gloves to be supplied by Grasse, and the tanners promoted themselves, showing an early appreciation of the importance of the right label. No longer humble artisans wrestling with buffalo hides, they now preferred to be thought of as *gantiers parfumeurs,* purveyors of perfumed gloves to the gentry.

All went well until the Revolution, when aristocrats and most of the trimmings of aristocratic life disappeared—the king, his dukes and counts, their private cooks and Parisian palaces, all sacrificed for the greater glory of the Republic. Not surprisingly, scented gloves, frivolous, elitist, and highly undemocratic, went too. The people of Grasse—by now quite attached to the idea of the label, and delighted to discover how flexible it could be—dropped any reference to gloves and simply called themselves *parfumeurs.* And perfume survived. Even in Revolutionary France, it was clear that not everyone wanted to smell like a Republican.

Today, some of the companies in Grasse make the perfumes they sell, but many others rely on the specialist talents of independent noses. This is big business, as we discovered when we arrived at Monsieur Ferrero's offices. The building is modern and, inside and out, looked as though someone had just been over it with a duster, buffing every surface to a high gloss. The air inside the building carried its own pleasant, very subtle scent—*eau de bureau,* perhaps—and the loudest noise was the sound of our footsteps on the marble floor as we followed Ferrero past calm, neat offices lined with bottles and computers.

"The creation of a perfume," he told us, "starts either with a brief from a client or a brainwave. In both cases, I begin with the *tableau olfactif,* the picture of the perfume in my head." He went on to develop the painting analogy, substituting nose for canvas and scents for colors. "How many different degrees of blue or pink are there? Hundreds. How many different degrees of citrus, or verbena, or jasmine? Thousands."

I think we saw most of them, and smelt a good many, in the course of the morning, until our noses were reeling. But the clear winner, in terms of making a memorable impression, was not a sublime floral essence or a miraculous mixture of herbs, but the kind of smell you would cross the street to avoid—a smell to bring tears to your eyes.

Ferrero took a taper, dipped it in a flask, waved it under my nose, and inclined his head. "This is quite remarkable," he said. "What do you think it is?"

It was foul; acrid, and strong enough to pucker the nostrils. But even I, a nasally challenged man if ever there was one, could recognize it. At least, I thought I could, although I hesitated to answer. It couldn't be what I thought it was—not here, not in this temple of fragrance.

"Well?" said Ferrero.

"Well," said I, "it seems familiar . . ."

"Another sniff?"

"No, no." I was still groggy from the first one. "It's most unusual. I'm just trying to . . ."

He held up a finger and put a stop to my floundering.

"*Pipi de chat,*" he said. "Entirely artificially made, with chemicals. Interesting, *n'est-ce pas?* Indistinguishable from the real thing."

Interesting wasn't the word I would have chosen to describe the smell of cat's urine, and I couldn't see immediately why it deserved a place in the *tableau olfactif,* but strange and wonderful are the ways of perfume artists. That same morning, I learned that whale vomit and goat musk—used sparingly, of course—also have their place in the creation of an irresistible scent. It's a question of how they react when mixed with other ingredients. And on that low note, we went to lunch.

Monsieur Ferrero was a delightful and informative companion, and even had the waiters eavesdropping as they served each course in an effort to pick up a little perfume wisdom. When I asked him the obvious question—why a tiny bottle filled mostly with water could cost as much as a bigger bottle filled with Château Latour—he shook his head.

"People have no idea," he said. "They think the price is high because of the expensive packaging, and of course that has something to do with it. But think of the ingredients we use." I did, and I'm ashamed to say that *pipi de chat* came to mind rather than attar of roses. "Essence of iris, for example, is now a hundred and ten thousand francs a kilo. And the cost of petals! You need ninety to a hundred thousand petals to make a single kilo of essence." He shrugged, spreading his hands in dismay at the investment required to keep us all sweet-smelling.

The second obvious question was how he knew when he had concocted a winner, and here computer technology and micro measurements took second place to feminine intuition. Or, as Ferrero put it, the wife test.

"I take home a little flacon of the new scent," he said, "and leave it where my wife will notice it. I say nothing. *Rien.* It is as though the flacon has arrived by magic. I wait. Still I say nothing. If the flacon is empty at the end of the week, that encourages me. If the flacon is still full, perhaps I think again. She has a good nose, my wife."

I had been keeping an eye on the Ferrero nose all through lunch, interested to see how it reacted to the stimuli provided by good wine and wild mushroom soup and the local specialty of cabbage stuffed with sausage and bacon, and I noticed one or two appreciative twitches. But it wasn't until the cheese tray was brought to the table that the nostrils began to flare in earnest, even though the tray was three feet away.

"If you like a strong cheese," he said, pointing to a creamy wedge with prominent dark blue veins that seemed to throb with cholesterol, "that is a *fromage détonateur.*"

So it was, one of the percussion instruments in the cheese orchestra, and it deserved another reflective glass of wine.

It's a curious job being a nose, and in one way must be rather unsatisfying. However you explain it—nature, luck, genes, years of application, an early formative encounter with *pipi de chat* or whale vomit—you are endowed with a great and unusual creative gift. Your nose in a million, your instincts, and your blending skills are the most important ingredients of perfumes that are slapped onto cheeks, dripped delicately onto bosoms, and dabbed behind hundreds of thousands of ears every day. And yet your work is signed by someone else: Yves Saint Laurent, Calvin Klein, Lagerfeld, Miyake, Chanel; never by you, the creator. You are that rare soul, the successful but anonymous artist, internationally unknown.

I thought how odd it must be to meet a stranger—man or woman, in an office or at a party—who smelled familiar, and how difficult it must sometimes be to restrain yourself from whispering: *It was I who made you smell the way you do.* I daresay you could get away with it in France, but probably not in America. Someone would inevitably sue you for nasal harassment.

Of all the small pleasures of the day, the best came last, when Ferrero gave me a copy of a letter he had written to the head of the perfume university in Versailles. It was to apply for a place on behalf of one of the blind students from Lardiers, a seventeen-year-old named David Maury who had shown exceptional promise. In fact, Ferrero wrote that he had been *"stupefait par l'acuité et la pertinence olfactives"* shown by the student. Coming from a professional, this is a powerful recommendation, and it looks as though the young nose will be accepted.

In Search of the Perfect Corkscrew

Last Christmas, an extravagant and well-meaning friend presented me with what he called a state-of-the-art corkscrew. It was a most serious piece of equipment—beautifully made, with what looked like a hydraulic leverage system. It was guaranteed to extract the most obstinate cork. My friend told me it was a connoisseur's corkscrew. He demonstrated it for me, and it did indeed remove the cork with the ease and smoothness one might expect from a modern triumph of alcoholic engineering. And yet it has never seen active service in our house. Not one more cork has it pulled; it still sits in its box, unused and unloved.

For an explanation of my apparent ingratitude, we need to go back to a summer lunch in a small village house not far from Avignon. I was the guest of Régis, a man who has for years kindly assumed responsibility for instructing me in the pleasures of the table. (It being well known, as he often reminded me, that any talent the English possess in matters of gastronomy is confined to breakfast and ripe Stilton.) Régis is not a cook, but describes himself as a gourmet/gourmand—that is, a knowledgeable and happily greedy student of the table, alert to every nuance in a recipe or a bottle. He claims that most of his adult life has been devoted to eating and drinking, and he has the stomach and expertise to prove it. He is also a practicing chauvinist, convinced that France leads the world in everything worthwhile.

Before we settled down to lunch, Régis had decided that we should exercise our palates—the only form of exercise he ever takes willingly—by comparing the virtues of two white wines from the Côtes-du-Rhone: a young Condrieu and an older, fatter Hermitage. There they sat, in twin buckets on the table, the bottles glistening with beads of chilled sweat. Régis rubbed his hands as he looked at them, twirled the bottles in their icy water, and then flexed his fingers with the air of a concert pianist about to do battle with Beethoven. Reaching into a trousers pocket, he pulled out a corkscrew, which he unfolded carefully.

With a graceful, practiced turn of the wrist, he passed a short, curved blade around the neck of the Condrieu, and the top of the capsule dropped off, a surgically neat cut with no rips or ragged edges. After drawing the cork, he held it to his nose, sniffed, and nodded. He repeated the process with the Hermitage, and was about to put the corkscrew back in his pocket when I asked to take a look at it.

Never had I seen such a handsome corkscrew. It was

based on the design of what is sometimes called The Waiter's Friend—blade at one end, lever at the other, screw in the middle. But there the resemblance stopped, because this was to ordinary corkscrews what Condrieu is to grape juice. It was a good weight in the hand, with a haft of polished horn, steel-tipped at each end. A spine of darker, patterned steel ran along the top of the handle, ending with a flat, stylized image of a bee. Stamped on the surface of the lever was the word Laguiole.

"That," said Régis, "is the best corkscrew in the world." He poured two glasses of wine, and grinned. "French, of course." And then, as we drank, he proceeded to fill the gaps in my corkscrew education.

Laguiole is a town in the Aveyron region of southern France, a town famous for knives. The ancestor of today's Laguiole corkscrews originated around 1880, following the invention of the cork. (In fact, corks had been introduced sometime before, in the eighteenth century, but nothing happens with breakneck speed in southern France.) Over the years, refinements such as stainless steel have been incorporated into the design, but little else has changed—not, at least, in the making of the genuine article.

Unfortunately, said Régis, it's a wicked, old world, and impersonations can be found everywhere: knives that resemble a Laguiole but which have been assembled by machine (this takes about an hour), and which are sold at much lower prices. The making of a *véritable Laguiole* involves around fifty separate operations, many of them carried out by hand. Each true knife is still put together by a craftsman instead of a machine, and each blade is stamped with an L. That's one sign of authenticity. There are others, traditional symbols of the elements: Water is represented by the wavy notches on the back of the blade;

air by the stylized bee; fire by the flame design running the length of the spine; and earth by a group of tiny brass nails—signifying grains of wheat—set into the handle. Without these, the knife in your hand may be sharp and handsome and even well made, but it won't be the real thing.

At this point Régis felt it was time for another demonstration, and reached for the bottle of Châteauneuf-du-Pape that would be supporting the cheese later on. "You see this?" he said, pointing to the short blade of the corkscrew. "A serrated edge. It cuts the capsule more cleanly than a straight edge, and it doesn't get blunt." He disposed of the capsule and pulled the cork. "Another thing," he said as he sniffed the cork thoughtfully. "You will observe that the screw is in the form of a *queue de cochon,* a pig's tail—hollow, and grooved so it won't split the cork. *Une merveille.* You must get one."

This led him to suggest an expedition. It was one of those frivolous plans that somehow make perfect sense when discussed over a long lunch. Together, said Régis, we would drive up to Laguiole and go shopping for my corkscrew, a purchase—no, an investment—that I would never regret. And while we were there, it would be unthinkable if we neglected to eat at the restaurant of Michel Bras, Laguiole's more recent claim to fame. Bras's restaurant is distinguished by four chef's toques and a nineteen out of twenty rating in the Gault Millau guide. Not only that, it is the spiritual home of the Gauloise Blonde. This, according to Régis, is a particularly aristocratic and delicious chicken, beside which other chickens are mere stringy sparrows. A queen among poultry. French, of course.

At the time, marinated in good wine as I was, the trip

seemed like an idea whose time had come, and I'm still not quite sure why we didn't set off the next day. Work intervened, I suppose, or perhaps Régis went for his liver's sake to take one of his periodic cures at Evian. But the idea was lodged in my mind, and my wife—not a student of corkscrews but certainly a connoisseur of chickens—was happy to come with me. Happier, in fact, than if I had gone with Régis, whom she considers a socially irresponsible companion. (It all goes back to the day I was late for dinner following a seven-hour lunch. It was a minor incident that took place many years ago, but wives have long memories.)

And so, one sharp, bright September morning, we left the Luberon and headed west, picking up the winding road that goes through the forests of the Cevennes. It was the same road that Robert Louis Stevenson had traveled with his donkey, and he would see little change in the surroundings today: mile after mile of wild countryside, green, beautiful, and empty. France has roughly the same population as Britain, but the inhabitants are spread over three times the land area, and in the Cevennes the spread is very thin. Apart from trucks loaded with tree trunks on their way to becoming roof beams, there was little traffic, and almost no sign of human habitation.

The road twists and turns too sharply to encourage overtaking, and after a while we didn't even try to pass the truck lumbering along in front of us with its load of pine trunks. By now it was close to noon, and we were wondering where in this magnificent isolation the driver would stop for lunch. Other nationalities may be content with a sandwich, but not the French, and certainly not the French *routier*. He wants to sit down at a table to eat in a civilized manner, and he will plan his journey accordingly.

In Search of the Perfect Corkscrew

Hungry people traveling in unfamiliar French territory will never go far wrong if they stick to this simple rule: At lunchtime, follow a truck. And so we did. Sure enough, it eventually led us off the road and into a parking area filled with other trucks. This we took to be the equivalent of a starred recommendation.

The building was low, functional, and noisy, the clientele almost entirely masculine. The menu, scrawled on a blackboard, listed *charcuterie,* cuttlefish poached in a saffron broth, cheese or dessert. The price of sixty-five francs included a bottle of wine. We sat outside, where the tables had been thoughtfully arranged to give every customer a view of the parking lot. Madame *la patronne,* surprisingly nimble for such an extremely large woman (in trucking terms, she would have been an eighteen-wheeler), somehow served lunch to more than forty people on her own without making anyone wait more than a few minutes. As we ate, we marveled at the efficiency, the standard of cooking, and the value for money to be found in the *relais routiers* network. Strange to think that this evening we would be having dinner at the other end of the restaurant ladder.

But before that, we had to change climates. The road became straighter and steeper, and by midafternoon we were driving through alpine countryside shrouded in cloud. Forest gave way to pasture, dotted with sleek caramel-colored cows glistening with moisture. Scattered villages came and went in the mist, the houses closed and shuttered, the streets deserted. There were more cattle than people. This was *la France profonde,* silent and rather eerie.

The hotel of Michel Bras came as a complete, almost shocking, contrast. We had been expecting a larger version of the village houses we had passed, something dark and thick-walled and traditional. What we found was an angular complex of stone and plate-glass buildings floating on top of a hill, all the more surreal because of the lack of visibility. It was like coming across a boat of the most contemporary design anchored in the clouds, far from land. Another surprise, when we checked in, was to find that we had the last available room. Out of season, in the middle of the week, in the middle of nowhere, the hotel was full. People come for the walking and the view, the young woman at the desk explained to us, with an apologetic shrug at the impenetrable curtain of gray outside the window. And, of course, the cooking.

But that was still a few hours away, and we drove the few miles back into Laguiole and, I hoped, the perfect corkscrew.

Laguiole is a small, pleasant town, and there is no doubt about its principal business. On the main street alone, there must be a dozen display windows bristling with knives: the classic pocket knife, the shepherd's friend (with an evil-looking spike at one end), dainty handbag-sized models for the modern woman. (What would she do with an accessory knife? Emergency manicures? Opening love letters? Puncturing a gentleman's reputation?) The variety of handles was astonishing—horn, rosewood, box, ebony, olive, and several woods I'd never heard of, like amourette, *bois de serpent,* and cocobolo. A knife-fancier's paradise.

The industry started with Pierre-Jean Calmels, who made the first Laguiole knife in 1829, and the shop in the main street bearing the family name seemed a likely place to find my corkscrew. Looking at the display cases, I saw knives and nothing but knives. And so I asked the woman behind the counter if she could show me such a thing as a corkscrew. This led to one of those French moments that every visitor experiences sooner or later when revealing an ignorance of local traditions or protocol. Disdain, first expressed by the eyebrows, then by a sigh, and finally by the tone of voice. "*Corkscrews?*" the woman said. "No. We make knives." She turned away to another customer, an elderly lady who was fingering a set of steak knives, testing their sharpness on the ball of her thumb. Finally, she made the decision to buy, nodded to herself, and justified the purchase: "Now I can give them cheaper meat," she said.

Chastened but determined, I went down the street, and found not only a corkscrew but something I could never have imagined: a knife with its own permanent and highly evocative aroma. This comes from the handle, a piece of wild Provençal juniper, a very fine-grained wood the color of dark honey. When rubbed by the fingers, it gives off the clean, strong scent of juniper and the *garrigue*. Close your eyes, said the salesman, and sniff. You could be in the mountains. Not only that, he added. This knife offers some unusual protective advantages too. Because juniper wood is a natural insect repellent, the pocket in which you keep your knife will stay forever free of moths, scorpions, or infestation by ants. That, I thought, is the kind of guarantee to give a man confidence as he makes his way through an insect-ridden world. Never again would I need to worry about termites in my trousers.

We crept back through the mist from Laguiole to the hotel, now fully lit and looking more than ever like a liner cruising in a dark sea, and went up to the main salon to have a drink before dinner. Granite and glass, fat armchairs of white leather, a central wood-burning fireplace that smelled not unlike the handle of my knife. In one corner, a Japanese couple, chic and shiny-haired, was being led through the joys of a long wine list by the sommelier. Behind us, the conversation was in German. The French customers were silent, noses sunk deep in their menus.

And now, with the drinks, came the pre-dinner ritual observed by every *restaurant de luxe*, the distribution of *amuse-gueules:* Tonight, there were tiny individual *cèpes* tarts, the pastry gauzy and crisp, and miniature pots of pâté, smooth as butter. I am never sure whether these small treats are to keep your strength up while struggling with the weight of the menu or to demonstrate the finesse of the cuisine, the chef's opening volley before he comes at you with the heavy artillery. The effect these mouthfuls had on me was to make me ravenous, my trucker's lunch forgotten as I looked through the day's selection.

It was a disappointment to see no mention of the celebrated chicken, who was obviously having an evening off, but her place was more than filled by fish, game, lamb, and beef, each dish described in short but succulent detail. I am always impressed by a well-written menu, one that is informative and appetizing without slipping into pretentious nonsense. Here, for example, is a London restaurant's attempt to justify the exorbitant price of its whitebait: *"The tiny fresh fish are tossed by our chef for a few fleeting seconds into a bath of boiling oil, and then removed before they have had a chance to recover from their surprise."* Anyone who suggests tossing the writer in after them has my full support.

There is none of that on the Michel Bras menu, and yet the brief phrases are filled with promise. It's quite an art, and I wondered if there was a professional menu-writer in the kitchen—perched on a stool in the corner, perhaps, glass of wine to hand, waiting to be inspired by events taking place in the ovens. All the great restaurants employ so many people in their kitchens that one more would hardly make a difference. And since most chefs are generous by nature, the writer might even be given a credit on the menu, somewhere in between the desserts and the *digestifs*. Stranger things have happened.

Small, expectant processions were now being led to their tables, and we saw that one of our fellow diners was being carried through in a large bag, small brown nose twitching in anticipation. We were pleased to see that Bras runs an equal opportunity establishment, where dogs are as welcome as their owners, and I tried to imagine the effect a dog would have in a top-class restaurant anywhere else in the world. Cries of alarm and calls to summon the public health inspector would just be the start of it, but here the bag and its hairy contents were quietly tucked away under the owner's chair without a single disapproving eyebrow being raised.

The room was long and elegant, with gray leather chairs, the tablecloths pulled tight and gathered underneath so that the round tables resembled oversized, opulent mushrooms. The cutlery, Laguiole's finest, had been specially designed. So had the table lamps. An endless supply of waiters came and went on silent feet, and there was more than a hint of reverence in the air. This is a characteristic of celebrated restaurants that can sometimes be overwhelming, causing voices to be muted and—for me, at least—threatening to turn a meal into some kind of minor religious experience. It's seldom the fault of the restaurant, but the deadening effect that excellence often has on the customers, who treat each exquisitely arranged plate like a shrine, forgetting that they came to have a good time as well as a good dinner. Laughter is the best background music.

And laughter we had, provided by the late arrival of ten boisterous French businessmen at the table next to ours. Stripping off their jackets before sitting down, they brought with them a breeze of informality and a clear determination to enjoy the evening. Toasts and jokes were made, insults exchanged, and lips were smacked as the first course appeared. Exceptional cooking seems to affect the French in two very different ways, and we saw examples of both at the tables around us. Our neighbors the enthusiasts were unrestrained in their appreciation, loud with pleasure; you could hear they loved what they were eating. In complete contrast, the chef-worshippers seemed to be in awe of every mouthful, chewing in respectful silence, nodding knowingly to each other in the manner of satisfied disciples as they identified the touch of cumin in one dish or the discreet squirt of truffle juice in another.

I'm all for the noisy enthusiast, and I suspect that most chefs like to hear that their work is appreciated. But gastronomic tradition in the great restaurants requires a degree of sanctity, particularly in the way food is presented. I remember one dinner in Paris where every plate of every course came to the table covered by a porcelain dome. There were four of us, and two waiters had been allocated to the table as dome-raisers. At a silent signal, the waiters swooped in to lift all four domes at precisely the same moment. It is a theatrical moment that can sometimes be embarrassing, as it was that night. The lamb chops I had ordered had lost their way and found a home elsewhere, leaving me with a plateful of salmon. You have to be careful with domes.

There was no risk of confusion *chez* Michel Bras. Our waiter slid through the tables with a giant silver tray raised to shoulder height, which he lowered to reveal undomed plates. A second waiter took charge of the plates and described each dish in exactly the same words that were used on the menu; a small courtesy for absent-minded gourmets, presumably in case there's a memory lapse in between the ordering of the dish and its arrival. All was impeccable, but before we had a chance to start, the waiter was back with a surprise we hadn't ordered—a glazed earthenware crock of something unfamiliar and white, giving off puffs of savory steam. He took a spoon, scooped and lifted. For a moment, spoon and dish were linked by a broad ribbon that the waiter twirled gracefully around the spoon before delivering a neat mound to the plate.

"This is special to our region," he said. "We call it *aligot.*"

I should warn you about *aligot.* It is wonderfully tasty, with a creamy texture and an impressive substance to it, almost as dense as toffee. It slips down so easily that it seems a crime not to have a second helping. Only sometime later are you aware of the unmistakable sensation that something is attaching itself firmly to your ribs.

Like many good things to eat and drink, *aligot* was made by monks—as long ago as the twelfth century, perhaps even before then. Pilgrims coming to the monastery in winter, cold and hungry, would ask if there was anything, or *aliquid,* to eat. The Latin *aliquid* became the French *aligot,* and the early recipe, basically melted cheese and breadcrumbs, was changed and refined. Today, this is what you need to make *aligot* for four:

Two pounds of potatoes; one pound of *tome d'Aubrac,*

the fresh local cheese; half a pound of sour cream; one or two cloves of garlic; salt and pepper. Boil and puree the potatoes, add the sour cream and cheese, stir as if your life depended upon it. If you have difficulty extracting the ladle from the saucepan, you've overcooked the recipe. Have a glass of wine and start again.

Aligot is the ideal restorative after eight hours of sustained manual labor in the fields, a day of skiing, or a fifteen-mile walk. Unfortunately, it tastes just as delicious if you have done nothing more physically demanding than change for dinner. It was odd to find such a solid peasant recipe in such a gastronomically sophisticated menu. Odd, and comforting; a reminder that food doesn't have to be complicated to be good.

Next morning the mist was as thick as *aligot*, with visibility limited to a few dank yards. Although we had been denied the view as well as the famous chicken, we were happy to have seen, so close to home, another country. The traditions, the cooking, the landscape, the accents, even the appearance of the people—all were completely different. Provence felt distant and exotic. It was hard to believe that we would be back there under sun and clear skies, among dark Mediterranean faces, within a few hours.

Meals inspire comparisons, not just of the food, but of the overall experience. What makes a restaurant memorable? What makes you want to go back to it, to recommend it? How does it achieve those coveted stars? As we drove down through the Cevennes we came to the conclusion that we would never qualify as Michelin inspectors; we'd fail the furniture appreciation test. In our experience, the Michelin guide only awards multiple stars to establishments that combine excellence of cooking with a certain level of decoration—you might call it *haut resto*—both in the equipment and the appearance of the staff. Chairs must be upholstered, and preferably specially designed. Waiters must be decked out in the restaurant livery. Sommeliers must wear ties. The financial investment in luxurious details—in crockery, table linen, glassware, cutlery, fresh flowers, elaborate menus, custom-made lighting— must be evident as soon as the customer (or the Michelin inspector) enters the room.

I'm sure this is all done with the best of intentions, and it clearly appeals to the French fondness for *apparence de richesse*. But it does tend to encourage the hushed, devout attitude, and an absence of what Régis likes to call *joie de manger*. All too often, the grand establishments suffer from a sad lack of gusto. It's true that you can't eat atmosphere. I don't care. I'd rather have dinner in a happy room than a reverent one, and to hell with the decorative trimmings.

Which brings me, with great pleasure, to the Auberge de La Môle, a restaurant that deserves at least three of my personal stars. It isn't in some of the major guides, possibly because of its straightforward approach to decor. At one time, it must have been a service station; a residual gas pump, now painted in blue and white, remains as an ornament on the terrace. Inside the entrance is a zinc bar polished by a thousand elbows, correctly equipped with assorted brands of pastis and a battery of those arcane aperitifs rarely found outside France. To reach the dining room, you walk through the kitchen, inhaling an aromatic prelude of what is to come: the scent of sauces and gravies, of grilling meat and roasting potatoes, and, in winter, of black truffles.

The dining room is simple, just this side of severe, with

a stone fireplace at one end. There is no attempt to be stylish or chic, nothing but the essentials—well-worn cutlery and tablecloths, unpretentious glasses, soft, faded napkins. The reassuring clatter of pots and pans comes from the kitchen as you contemplate the menu.

This won't take long. The first course and the last two courses are selections—generous selections, as we shall see—and they come to your table without any decision on your part. All you are required to do is choose your main dish from half a dozen suggestions, and to exercise whatever restraint you can summon up in the matter of wines. The Raynal family has been running the Auberge for forty years, and one Raynal after another has worked diligently to build a formidable cellar. There are excellent local wines from the Var, at forty or fifty francs a bottle, sharing the long list with venerable works of art from Burgundy and Bordeaux at two or three thousand francs. Let your wallet be your guide.

Before our first visit to the Auberge, friends familiar with the cooking had warned us against too much enthusiasm during the early part of the meal. Pace yourselves, they had told us, or you'll have to be carried out. But on that particular night it was cold and we were famished. We were also curious to see just how good the chef was, which naturally required us to taste everything. Some may call this gluttony; I like to think of it as dutiful research. We tucked our napkins under our chins. Even the wood smoke from the fire smelled appetizing.

Toast came first, but not in thin, limp, Anglo-Saxon slices. This was country bread cut thick, crisp and lightly browned on each side, warm and soft in the middle, edible transport for the terrines that were now arranged across the table. There were four of them—deep rectangular pottery dishes, their contents ranging in texture and complexion from smooth and pale to chunky and dark, from pork to hare. A knife was stuck unceremoniously into each block of pâté. A jar of cornichons, those tiny, pungent French cousins of the American pickle, was set in front of us, and we were left to help ourselves.

There had been a murmured word of warning from the young girl serving us. An extra dish, she said, had been prepared tonight, wild mushrooms, gathered that morning. The chef would be serving them in a case of light pastry. We were advised to save some room. But it was easier said than done. There is something about homemade pâtés and good warm bread that encourages lengthy and thorough comparison. Is the pork as good as the hare? Or better? Opinion changes with each mouthful, and so one has to try again, slipping in a cornichon from time to time to punctuate the different flavors. Only the arrival of the mushrooms prevented us from making an entire meal out of the first course.

Our friends had told us about a faithful admirer of the restaurant, an elderly gentleman who turned up every week to eat Sunday lunch alone. He came by taxi from Toulon, a distance of forty miles or so, and his taxi waited outside during the two hours it took him to do justice to the menu before driving him back home. In other parts of the world, such gastronomic devotion might be considered unusual. But the French go out of their way to support their stomachs and their chefs, which is why you can often find extraordinary cooking in the most unlikely corners of the countryside.

There is an interesting theory about hunger—and we were finding it to be true—which goes something like this: After a certain amount of any one food, you become sated.

But with a change of flavor and a change of texture, your appetite revives in the most magical fashion. Thus it was with the next course, a confit of duck and a circular, golden-brown cake of potatoes. Layers of them, sliced thin, roasted in duck fat and "encouraged," as the chef said, by the addition of garlic and chopped truffles. This, combined with the confit, would probably carry a health warning on more nutritionally correct menus—a cardiologist's nightmare, seething with cholesterol, a virtual guarantee of an early grave. But for once, we said to ourselves as we mopped up the last of the gravy, we had statistics on our side. As it happened, there were several living statistics in the restaurant, men and women of advanced age and youthful appetite, testimony to the fact that France has one of the lowest rates of fatal coronary heart disease in the western world. Not for the first time, we raised our glasses to the French Paradox.

Sustained by that thought, but by now beginning to flag, we were presented with a platter the size of a manhole cover: cheeses, from hard to soft to almost liquid. Most of them had come straight from the farmer without passing through the sterilization processes so dear to the hearts of the food censors in Brussels (sometimes described as the bland leading the bland), and consequently tasted good enough to be illegal. They probably were.

And then, a pause. A chance to catch the breath, adjust the napkin, and gather strength for the chef's parting shots—not one, not two, but three desserts: a small hot apple tart, a deep dish of crème caramel, and a bowl of pears simmered in red wine. Finally, coffee and a nip of Calvados.

I asked if there was any chance of a cigar. A basket piled

high with boxes was brought in from the cellar—Partagas and Cohibas, even those rare, fat No. 2 Montecristos, the great Cuban torpedoes. Havanas were served as generously as dinner had been, laid on the table in abundance for you to take your pick. The one I chose was in perfect condition, the Calvados had the proper whiff of apples, we were at peace with the world. L'Auberge de La Môle, we agreed, was the kind of restaurant the French do better than anyone else: highly professional, and yet it felt like the extension of a friend's kitchen, casual, easy, and comfortable. The restaurants with a row of stars, as good as they are, tend to have a similar veneer, polished, perfect, and international. The Auberge couldn't be anything but French.

Less than twenty miles from St.-Tropez, the restaurant has had its share of summer celebrities who come to sit and eat in plastic chairs by the gas pump on the terrace. The Princess of Wales, the two Jacks (Chirac and Nicholson), Joan Collins, and a blonde sprinkling of Riviera girls, *les mimis de St.-Tropez*—almost famous, tanned to their toenails and accompanied by their elderly uncles. During August, the parking area next to the restaurant looks as though the local Porsche and Mercedes dealers are having a convention. Cell phones, titanium-framed sunglasses, and Vuitton beach bags litter the tables. Inside, at the bar, their backs to the glamour, local farmers and workmen argue about football or the Tour de France. And then they go home to lunch.

Eight Ways to Spend
a Summer's Afternoon

Of the many questions in life that I prefer to duck, one of the most frequent comes from that daunting creature, the serious traveler seeking advice. He—it's almost always a man, for some reason—is not the kind to take his pleasures lightly. He approaches his vacation as though making a business trip without the customary protection of suit and tie and personal assistant, and he is profoundly suspicious of the random expedition or the unplanned moment. Gaps in his itinerary cause him to fidget until they are plugged, and the thought of anything being left to chance is enough to give him grave doubts about his secretary's efficiency. He is the spiritual descendant of those package-tour pioneers who used to take pride in doing Europe in five days. And when considering a visit to Provence, his first question, asked by phone and inevitably confirmed by fax, is: When is the *best* time to come?

I try to fend him off with questions of my own. Does he want to see the poppies and cherry blossoms of spring? Does he want to roast himself in the peak sunbathing season of July and August? Take in the Avignon festival of music and drama? Ride a bicycle up Mont Ventoux? Run naked through the Luberon? Tread the grapes—vicariously, of course—during the autumn days of the *vendange*, and see the vines begin to turn rusty gold? Does he have architecture and Roman remains on his agenda, or antiques markets and three-star restaurants?

Yes, he says, yes. I like the sound of everything. But I only have a week to fit it all in. So when is the *best* time to come?

I have struggled to find an answer, or at least an answer that will satisfy him; and I have failed, miserably and often. The closest I can get—a recommendation arrived at after years of haphazard research—is not a convenient string of days that can be blocked off in a diary. I suppose it's more of an attitude of mind than a precise arrangement of dates and places, and is therefore often received by the serious traveler in puzzled silence. Provence, I tell him, is at its best after lunch.

A summer lunch for preference, because the first of two simple requirements for maximum enjoyment is sunshine. The second is a total absence of fixed plans. Only then can you take full advantage of the long and unencumbered afternoon that lies ahead.

The bill is paid, the last mouthful of rosé swallowed, the empty bottle upended in the ice bucket as a farewell salute to the waiter. Now is the time to review the possibilities, taking into account the temperature, your energy level, and the nature of your inclinations—sporting, intellectual, cultural, or physical. (Another glass of wine is not a bad idea here, purely for inspirational purposes.) Despite the lack of theme parks, multiscreen cinemas, and shopping malls, Provence is not short of diversions. And while the selection that follows is highly personal, I hope it will serve to illustrate my belief that this is the best place in the world to amuse yourself doing almost nothing.

A Ringside Seat at a Game of Boules

Almost every village possesses its own modest version of the sports arena. At its most basic, this is nothing more than a level patch of land perhaps twenty or thirty meters long with a dusty surface of gravel and hard-packed earth. If it is a well-established athletic facility—one, let's say, that has been in service for a couple of hundred years— you are likely to find two additional refinements. The first is shade, provided by an orderly parade of plane trees that might have been planted by one of Napoléon's military gardeners. The second is refreshment, available from the café that overlooks the playing area. (This is often called Le Sporting, and will usually have a row of *boules* trophies, bulbous and gleaming, on the shelf behind the bar.)

Variations on the game of *boules* have been in existence ever since man discovered the delights of throwing a ball at a target that can't throw back. Early versions of the *boule* itself have now become, like wooden tennis rackets and hickory-shafted golf clubs, sporting antiques. They are wonderfully handsome objects, made from nails that have been hammered into a boxwood core to form a sphere, the nail heads so tightly packed that they resemble scales on a fish. Pleasing to look at and satisfying to hold, their fault is that, being handmade and slightly uneven in shape, they are inclined to skip away from the true line once they hit the ground. In a game where millimeters count and passions run high, this skittish behavior was the cause of much grief and argument, and eventually the old *boule* was replaced by the perfectly engineered, perfectly round steel missile we see today.

This doesn't mean to say that grief and argument have disappeared from the game. Indeed, grief and argument, as much as precision and skill, are essential to the enjoyment of both players and spectators, adding drama to what might otherwise merely be a well-behaved series of lobs.

The purpose of the contest is to place your group of *boules*—knocking others out of the way if necessary—as close as possible to the target, a small wooden ball called the *cochonnet*. Once the players have thrown, they walk up the court to take measurements. A simple matter, you might think, one that can be carried out in a sportsman-like fashion, abiding by the principle of May the Best Man Win. But no. Not a bit of it. The players huddle over their *boules* in a fever of dispute, debating every hairsbreadth of distance from the *cochonnet*, arms, voices, and sometimes pocket rulers raised in triumph or disbelief. May the Loudest Man Win.

It is possible that these regular outbursts of discord are inspired by something more than the honest quest for victory; something a little stronger. *Boules*, as far as I know, is unique in the world of outdoor athletic competition. You can drink while you're playing. You don't even have to put down your glass when you throw, providing you possess reasonable physical coordination and a steady hand. And I have often thought that alcohol may account for some of the uninhibited and quite remarkable techniques displayed by the game's stylists.

The throw itself, an underhand pitch of either high or low trajectory, is normally a study in disciplined concentration, knees bent, eyes fixed on the target. It is the follow-up where individual flourishes come into play, a kind of curious ballet that is conducted on the spot, since the player is supposed to stay behind the throwing line. There he stands, often on one leg, his body leaning forward, back, or sideways, depending on the flight of the throw, his flapping arms acting either as accelerators urging the *boule* on or brakes willing it to slow down, his single earthbound foot on tiptoe. The effect is not unlike a heron trying to take off from a river bed with one leg stuck in the mud. It is a sight to make you smile as you sit in the shade watching the puffs of dust raised by the *boules*, the clunk of steel against steel (like the gnashing of a dinosaur's teeth) mingling with the ebb and flow of argument and the tinny thump of the café radio. The players move slowly from one end of the court to the other, and back again. The air is hot and still. Time stops.

One of the charms of *boules* is that it can be played, badly but enjoyably, by an amateur of almost any age. Brute force is less important than cunning and a good eye, and I find it odd that the game seems to be reserved exclusively for men. In all my years as an idle spectator, I have never seen a Frenchwoman step up to the mark during the course of these sessions that run into the early evening. Curiosity once made me ask a couple of old experts why their wives didn't join them on the court. One dismissed the question with a shrug. The other scarcely hesitated. "Don't be ridiculous," he said. "Who would cook dinner?"

Wet Gardening

I am not blessed with the essential attribute of the successful gardener, which is patience—the ability to take the long view, to pace myself according to the speed of the seasons, to wait for years before the sprig grows into a mature and recognizable form. I also have a physical disability: My thumb is not the traditional gardener's green, but a dingy, rather sinister brown. Others seem able to touch an ailing shrub and restore it to the fine green glow of health. My attentions—well-meant but clearly not well-received—achieve the reverse. A week in my care is enough to reduce a normally robust bloom to a state of wilting despair. Plants see me coming, and shrivel.

This will partly explain why I feel that a garden in Provence is my kind of garden. The climate is cruel, with temperatures that dip below freezing and rise above 100 degrees. The earth is rocky rather than rich, water comes in torrents or not at all, and when the mistral blows it exfoliates the landscape, tearing off the topsoil and battering everything in its path. Experience has taught me that any vegetation capable of surviving in these hostile conditions can survive even my best efforts.

Among my acquaintances are one or two keen gardeners. Intoxicated by horticultural terminology, they have a casual yet scholarly way of referring to the inhabitants of their gardens in Latin. To them, buttercups and daisies are *Ranunculus acris* and *Leucanthemum vulgare,* and the modest dandelion is promoted to *Taraxacum officinale.* I cope with these displays of expertise with uncomprehending nods, or by trying to change the subject, but they won't be distracted. And it isn't long before they begin to offer advice on how I could transform my arid plot of Provence into a transplanted English cottage garden.

A little color would be nice, they say, looking around them with mild disapproval. Something to brighten the place up. And a *lawn*. There's nothing quite as restful to the eye as a lawn (amazingly, it doesn't appear to have a Latin name). From the imaginary lawn, it is only a short step to espaliered fruit trees, rose bowers, flowering hedges, and those essential living ornaments so dear to the English heart, herbaceous borders. One of these days they will suggest ha-has and parterres. I can feel it coming.

It's a relief when they go and I am left to look at what I love: lavender and cotton lavender, cypress, sage, rosemary, bay, oleander, box, thyme. Grays from almost blue to almost white, greens from shiny and dark to dusty and faded, a summer splash of purple, colors and shapes that suit the landscape, plants that conquer the climate and tolerate me. They need very little to sustain them, and the only major duty is more of a pleasure than a chore: the cutting of the lavender in July.

This is best done wet. You soak yourself in the pool before taking up the sickle or the secateurs to start the first row. The stalks are dry, almost brittle, and cut cleanly. After gathering a few clumps, your hands take on the scent of fresh lavender, sharp and astringent. Within five minutes the sun has dried the last drop of water from your body; within ten minutes you're sweating. At the end of half an hour, another trip to the pool and a flop into heaven.

An afternoon of this will give you a pile of cut lavender, with a dozen ways to enjoy it. The fragrance lives to an aromatic old age, and a small sachet of lavender left in a drawer or linen closet in July will retain its scent, faded but still distinctive, until December or beyond. A stalk or two in bottles of olive oil or vinegar is an infusion of summer that lasts the whole year. And then there is lavender essence, the Provençal cure-all. Use a few drops as a disinfectant on scratches or insect bites, as a gargle to soothe a sore throat, as an inhalant in a bowl of hot water to clear a thick head, as a scorpion repellent when you swab down the kitchen floor. Finally, save a few bunches of dried lavender to put on to the first fires of winter, and the house will smell like the purple patch you cut those many months ago. Try getting all that out of a herbaceous border.

Rendezvous with an Artisan

An old house—built before the arrival of preformed doors and windows, instant kitchens, and the many other dubious delights of modern modular construction—is at the same time a joy and a constant obstacle course. What you gain in character you lose in architectural perfection. Floors have slopes and develop mysterious swellings in winter. Walls tilt. Doorways list to one side. Stairs lurch upward with little regard for regularity, and the true right angle is nowhere to be found. And so, when the time comes to replace a sagging banister, a worm-eaten door, or a warped shutter, it is impossible to find a ready-made substitute. You must brace yourself for a series of encounters with that amiable and talented will-of-the-wisp, the Provençal artisan. He will make whatever your heart desires.

Scores of artisans are at your disposal throughout the

Vaucluse, masters of their various crafts. But whether they work their magic in wood, pottery, stone, marble, wrought iron, or steel, they all seem to share similar characteristics. These become apparent during the course of the job, revealing themselves according to the number of visits that you make. And a summer's afternoon, when lunch has made you sufficiently benign to look upon the whole process as a form of entertainment, is as good a time as any to make a start.

Your first visit will almost certainly include a guided tour of the atelier, where you will be invited to admire commissions undertaken for other clients. Marvelous half-finished objects litter the workshop floor, and you feel fortunate to be in the presence of an artist who can make exactly, precisely, what you want. Not only that; he is encouragingly eager for your business, ready to drop everything and come to your house to take measurements, maybe that very same evening.

At the house, details are noted in the curling pages of a weather-stained exercise book. There are, of course, complications that you, an innocent in these matters, couldn't be expected to understand without a short lecture. Irregularities and difficulties are revealed to you, the ravages of rust and decay pointed out with many a sad shake of the head. A delicate and sympathetic touch is needed, but you are reassured that you have found the man for the job. *Pas de problème.* A price is quoted and agreed upon, and then you plunge into the realm of the unknown by asking when he might be able to deliver. He counters by asking when you would like that to be. You think of a date, add on a month, and tell him.

This is the cue for the artisan's motto, which I have heard so often that I think it must be taught to every young apprentice on his first day at work. In response to your suggestion of a delivery date, there will be a short silence followed by an intake of breath and a thoughtful nod. *C'est possible,* he will say. You will notice that he hasn't actually said yes, merely that what you ask is not beyond the bounds of possibility. It is a subtle but important distinction, as you will discover. However, for the moment you feel that the two of you have come to a clear and businesslike arrangement.

Not wishing to appear like an aggressive and impatient foreigner, you let a decent interval elapse before calling to check on the job's progress. It will be an unsatisfactory conversation—if you can call it a conversation—because the artisan's telephone is always situated in the loudest corner of his workshop, the area of maximum din. I'm sure this is a deliberate tactic designed to scramble unwelcome questions of a specific nature, or maybe it's a recording that cuts in automatically. Anyway, it works. Nobody can talk for long to a wall of noise made by a buzz saw or a stonecutter or an enthusiastic welder in full cry. A few half-words might penetrate the clatter, bang, and screech, but not enough to make any sense, and so the seeker after truth is obliged to make another personal visit.

Nothing much has changed in the atelier. The same marvelous objects are still there, still half-finished. If you're lucky, another one—yours—will have joined the collection, and this will be shown to you with the pride of a father introducing a favorite daughter. It's beautiful, just what you had hoped for. Is there any chance, you ask, of having it next week?

The intake of breath, the thoughtful nod. *C'est possible.*

Of course, it won't be ready. But what the hell. The house isn't going to fall down without it.

Shopping

I would be interested to know if any research has been done on the connection between a well-served stomach and a few glasses of wine and the urge to go forth and acquire. I am not by nature a shopper, and the idea of trailing around on the lookout for something I don't need has no appeal for me—except when I've had a good lunch. It is then, in the early afternoon, replete, good-humored, and expansive, that I become a willing and susceptible mark; a consumer, ready to consume. In cities, this has occasionally led to expensive embarrassments and stern words from American Express. I'm safer in Provence, where there is a nostalgic fondness for cash.

Many of our neighbors are avid collectors and supporters of *petits fournisseurs*—the small, unadvertised suppliers who grow or make their own products and, ignoring chain stores and supermarkets, sell directly to the public. Their headquarters, *les bonnes adresses,* are usually lost in the countryside or tucked away in the backstreets, simple and inconspicuous, hard to find without directions. The specialty of the house might be anything from white anchovies to custom-made espadrilles, but whatever it is will not be sold to you without a bonus. Education is included in the price—a dash of history, a few remarks on the manufacturing process, and a generous measure of self-promotion, with the occasional sly swipe at mass-produced competition. In other words, the customer should not be in a hurry. This is how I like shopping to be, and a slow, hot afternoon is when I like to do it.

We had been given an address in Cavaillon where one could find the ultimate melon, a melon whose exquisite bouquet and ravishing juiciness were only matched by the erratic and often disagreeable nature of the proprietor. It sounded like an interesting combination, and after some geographical difficulties we found ourselves in a cul-de-sac on the edge of town, not far from the main produce market.

The little street was deserted, quiet enough to hear the flies that had gathered in a buzzing cloud around the open doorway of what might once have been a stable. The pervasive smell of sweet ripe fruit was in the air, and a white Mercedes was parked in the shade opposite the open door. It must belong to a prosperous customer, I thought. He's probably inside haggling with the old melon king, a peasant from the fields, appropriately gnarled and dusty.

We pushed our way through the flies and stood on the threshold of a dim, perfumed space almost entirely filled with yellow-green melons piled on a thick bed of straw. Seated at a scarred metal table just inside the entrance, a man was snarling into a portable phone, his language adding to the ripeness of the atmosphere. He was slight and dark, with strands of black hair pulled across a tanned pate, a neat mustache under a sharp nose that supported wraparound sunglasses. A striped, open-necked shirt, iridescent dark-blue trousers, black shoes with vaguely equine brass snaffles decorating each instep—could this natty apparition be the melon king?

He finished his conversation with a grunt and reached for a cigarette before turning his sunglasses toward us. "We'd like to buy some melons," I said, "and we've heard that yours are the best."

Perhaps the compliment was enough to make him amiable; or perhaps he, too, was still under the influence of lunch. But he stood up politely and waved his cigarette at the massed display behind him. "These," he said, "are the best of the best, the Charentais *sublimes*, the favorite melons of Alexandre Dumas the elder. But of course," he said, "that is well known." He picked up the end of a coiled hose and turned a fine spray of water on to the piles banked up against the back wall. I had the feeling that this was step one in the melon salesman's manual, because it emphasized the scent of the fruit, heady and moist and dense. He selected one, pressed the base with his thumb and sniffed the top before passing it over to me and turning to look in a corner behind his metal table.

The melon felt surprisingly heavy for its size, the skin freckled with beads of water, the stem end slightly soft. We inhaled and made admiring noises. The melon king smiled, his expression at odds with the eighteen-inch machete he had found in the corner. "Now you must see the flesh," he said, taking back the melon. A flick of the blade, and it was in two halves, vivid orange, brimming with juice, a treat that he told us would "charm the throat and cool the belly." (I later found out that he had borrowed the line from a melon-fancier who was also a poet, but it was most impressive at the time.)

Demonstration over, he looked at us expectantly. "I can quote you a good price per ten kilos," he said, "with a discount if you take more than a *tonne*. But you must arrange transportation." His eyebrows appeared above his sunglasses, hovering in wait for the order.

How were we to know? Our friends hadn't told us that he was a *grossiste*, a wholesaler, a man who shipped thousands of *tonnes* of melons to the best tables in Paris every summer. To his credit, and contrary to his reputation, he let us buy a dozen, throwing in a handful of damp straw to line the shallow wooden box which he gave us to carry them away.

We stopped at a café before going back to the car, and found that we had another melon expert in our waiter. The thing to do, he told us, was to cut off the top, scoop out the seeds, pour a bottle of vodka into the hollow, and leave the melon in the fridge for twenty-four hours. The vodka is soaked up by the flesh of the melon, making a potent dessert of unimaginable delicacy.

Something to charm the throat and cool the belly?

"*Voilà*," he said. "*Exactement.*"

A Museum to Drive You to Extraction

Is there any other country in the world that has a frog fair or a snail festival? An official celebration of the sausage? A special day dedicated to garlic? Where else but France could you find cheeses, sea urchins, oysters, chestnuts, plums, and omelettes honored by a blaze of local limelight that in other countries would be reserved for victorious football teams or national lottery winners?

It should have come as no surprise, therefore, when news reached me of a museum devoted to that noble and necessary tool, the corkscrew. After all, in a country where the making and drinking of wine is regarded as one of the more civilized religions, it seems only fair that some recognition is given to the implement that uncorks the pleasures of the bottle. But an entire museum? It must be tiny, I thought, a midget among museums, with a few dozen corkscrews that had been discovered in the attic of an acquisitive ancestor. I wasn't expecting a miniature Louvre.

In fact, the museum is only part of a transformation that has taken place on the D188 just below Ménerbes. This used to be a stretch of road much like dozens of others in the valley. There was an old farmhouse set in fields of vines on one side, and Monsieur Pardigan's garage (guarded by two geese) on the other—a few hundred meters of unremarkable countryside, pleasant enough, but nothing to make you slow down, let alone stop.

Now the garage and the geese are gone, and the farmhouse has sprouted wings and annexes, built with such sympathy and cunning that it's difficult to see where the old ends and the new begins. The vines have been groomed, with rose bushes planted at the end of each row. A short avenue of century-old olive trees leads from the road to the building. Wherever you look, you see evidence of a tasteful eye and a generous budget.

The man behind this recasting of the countryside, Yves Rousset-Rouard, is the current mayor of Ménerbes. An interest in wine led him one day to the Drouot auction rooms in Paris, where one of the lots was a collection of corkscrews. He bought them, fascinated by their variety and by their history. He bought more, and became known to other collectors and dealers. He continued to buy. He's still buying. Now he has hundreds of corkscrews, all different. A nightmare to store—unless you happen to own a vineyard, a *cave*, and a handsome building in which to keep your hobby.

You will see a hint of what is to come in the tasting room. Lying on a wooden table is a giant's corkscrew, three feet long if it's an inch, requiring both hands to lift, a bottle of several gallons to do it justice, and a muscular assistant to help with the extraction—far too big to be displayed in the vitrines of the museum itself. This you will find beyond the tasting room, an austere, elegant space, as dim as a church, the only light coming from dozens of glass-fronted cabinets recessed into the walls.

And there they are, more than a thousand corkscrews, each with a brief description of its origin and its place in corkscrew history. It is a testament to man's love affair with the bottle, and his ingenuity in turning a functional tool into a decorative, humorous, whimsical, occasionally lewd accessory. The corkscrew as a phallus, the corkscrew operated by the closing of a pair of female legs, the corkscrew as part of a pistol or a hunting knife, the corkscrew concealed in a walking stick or attached to what appears to be a set of brass knuckles—every embellishment you can imagine, presented in the atmosphere of a jewelry showroom. (Appropriately enough, a Bulgari corkscrew is among the exhibits.) Handles made from horn, olive wood, bakelite, a deer's foot, or the effigy of Senator Volstead, the father of Prohibition; folding corkscrews, vest-pocket corkscrews, an example—one of only three known to be in existence—of the earliest corkscrew, and its more elaborately engineered twentieth-century descendant; and, as if this incomplete list of attractions weren't enough, it is the only museum I know where you can get a drink. Even better, you're *encouraged* to have one.

Back in the tasting room, blinking in the late afternoon light, it is very pleasant to spend half an hour sampling the wines made on the property, and perhaps toasting one man's obsession. Not surprisingly, you can even buy a corkscrew.

Planning Your Own Château

We never seem to tire of rummaging through the contents of strangers' attics, and *brocante* markets, selling everything from chamber pots to grandma's old armoire, do a brisk business throughout Provence. But market-hopping is not without its dangers. Picking through those stalls can become addictive, often leading to what an American friend calls antiques escalation—the search for bargains that are so enormous you need a truck to take them away. Why settle for the contents of a house when you can buy the house itself, or at least great chunks of it? The official term is architectural salvage, and there is, on the outskirts of Apt, a wonderful example of it, a repository where you can spend a happy hour or two mentally constructing the château of your dreams.

The Chabaud brothers, Henri and Jean, occupy several acres of what appears to be an ancient city in ruins. Whenever I go there, it is with modest intentions—to find a cast-iron chimney back, an old stone garden tub, a few handmade tiles. But it doesn't take long before these are forgotten, and I find myself entertaining ideas well above my wallet, as impractical as they are grandiose.

This time, delusions of nobility start to occur just inside the entrance, set off by the sight of a reclining amphora balanced on the bulge of its stomach. It is large enough to engulf a tall man, a good seven feet in length, with an opening wider than my shoulders. It would look magnificent in the garden, at the end of an allée of cypress trees. But what would we put in it? Three tons of earth and some geraniums? A guest who overstayed his welcome? I delegate that problem to the imaginary head gardener, and move on.

In the distance I can see something else that would add a personal touch to the domestic environment: an entire gateway, stone columns joined by a stone arch, hung with ornate iron doors. Coming closer, I see that the address has been chiseled into the arch. Château Lachesnaye, in emphatic capital letters. Now all we need is the château to go with it.

The elements are all here, even if fitting them together might take a lifetime: tiles for the roof, flagstones for the floors, monumental cut-stone fireplaces, oak beams, pediments, Palladian columns, and staircases for every destination—straight ahead, curving to the left, or curving to the right. The scale of almost everything is gigantic, more suited to basketball players than the original owners of the seventeenth and eighteenth centuries. People were smaller in those days. Did they enjoy being dwarfed by their living rooms? Did they need maps to find their way through the corridors and antechambers? Did they ever mislay their servants in the maze of attics and garrets?

The sun is fierce, and I sit in the shade next to a curious statue of a woman with a prominent bosom who has inexplicably turned into a lion from the waist down. Looking past her I can see a middle-aged couple with a younger man, whom I take to be their architect. He has just finished measuring a very old, very fine fireplace.

"Too big for the room," he says.

"Nonsense," says his client. "We'll just cut it down to fit."

The architect winces, his feelings written on his face. Here is a beautiful, perfectly proportioned piece of stone furniture that has somehow survived all the pillage and destruction of the past two hundred years or so, from the aftermath of the French Revolution to World War II. Now it is in danger of being sacrificed to fill a nook.

Beyond the group around the fireplace, a staircase as wide as a room rises fifteen feet before ending in thin air, with a cat dozing on the top step. Crumbling grandeur stretches as far as the eye can see, and I wonder about life in a château. What would it have been like, spending your days in one of these extravagant stone caves? Once the thrill of having a dining room the size of a football field had worn off, realities would have to be faced, particularly the winter: no central heating, rising damp, spartan hygienic arrangements, inadequate lighting, food grown cold during its long voyage from the kitchen to the table—very similar, as it happens, to life in one of England's more expensive boarding schools.

Not for me. Not this afternoon, at any rate. Châteaux are at their best in the permanent summer of the imagination, and that's probably where mine will stay.

A Guided Tour of the Housing Shortage

After a week or two in Provence, you will have had plenty of sun, wandered through a dozen markets, visited vineyards, paid your respects in churches, and sat on a piece of ancient history in the orchestra stalls of a Roman theater. In other words, you will have seen what any active, curious tourist sees. Now, perhaps, you would like to see a little more; you'd like to see how the natives live. In fact, you'd love to have a good look around some of their houses.

Other people's houses fascinate us, and if the other people and their houses are in a foreign country, they somehow have an extra fascination. When you're invited to see one, small details catch the eye: Titles on the spines of books run the wrong way. The brands of everything from soap to refrigerators have unfamiliar names. Windows open inward instead of outward. There are wooden shutters in those marvelously faded colors, stone fireplaces, vaulted rooms. The house even smells different.

It's all faintly exotic. You find yourself thinking how delightful it would be to have a home away from home, here in Provence. And what more pleasant way to pass a free afternoon than to inspect a selection of charming possibilities?

Enter the real estate agent.

While I don't have exact figures, it certainly appears that *agents immobiliers* in the Luberon are almost as numerous as bakers. In every village large enough to have its own fête and official parking lot, there seems to be at least one boutique-sized office, its window glowing with seductive photographs: tiny ruins ripe for conversion, farms with cherry orchards and twenty-mile views, *bastides* and *maisons de maître* and *bergeries,* entire hamlets— there they are, sitting in the sun and waiting for the loving touch of a new proprietor. What a choice!

The agent is most happy to see you, and how wise you were to bypass his competitors and come to him first. Although you wouldn't think it from the selection in his window, there is, as he explains, a shortage of attractive properties in the Luberon. But he is remarkably fortunate in having the pick of them on his books, and it will be his pleasure to escort you to them personally.

At this point you might run into a snag. In an effort to be considerate, you say to him that you'd prefer just to see the location of three or four promising houses before taking a tour of any interiors. You have a car and a map. If he would tell you where to find the properties, you wouldn't have to take up his valuable time or bother the owners unnecessarily.

Mais non. That, unfortunately, will not be possible, and here is where you learn lesson number one. All kinds of excuses may be given for declining your thoughtful suggestion, but you've already heard the reason. There is a shortage of attractive properties in the Luberon. However, there is no shortage of real estate agents; in fact, there's a glut of them, and it's a situation that leads to intense competition. When a single property is given to three or four agents, as is often the case, the agent who introduces the property to the eventual purchaser is well placed to claim the commission (which is healthy: five percent or more of the purchase price). First come, first paid is the rule. That is why the escorted visit is crucial. It enables the agent to mark the territory.

Lesson number two: Such is the level of suspicion and secrecy that the most obvious and innocent question can provoke miracles of evasion. Let's say you have seen a house advertised in *Côté Sud,* the glossy magazine of the South, and you like the look of it. You call the agent whose name is at the bottom of the advertisement.

YOU: I wonder if you could tell me a little about one
of your properties—the reference is F2637.
AGENT: *Ah, un charme fou!*
YOU: Yes, it looks very nice. Where is it?
AGENT: Come to my office, and I can show you all
the photographs.
YOU: I'm sure. But where exactly is the house?
AGENT: It's between St. Rémy and Avignon, only
forty-five minutes from the airport . . .
YOU: But where? [The area mentioned is large
enough to hide an army, let alone a house.]
AGENT: . . . with a ravishing view of the Alpilles from
one of the upstairs windows . . .
YOU: Close to a village?

AGENT: . . . facing south to catch all the sun, in fact
   gorgée de soleil, secluded, but not isolated . . .
YOU: Which village?
AGENT: . . . and if you'd like to make a rendezvous, I
   can take you to see it tomorrow.

And so it goes on. The agent will go into rhapsodies
about the Roman roof tiles, the courtyard, the two-
hundred-year-old plane trees, and the wine cellar. He will
tell you about the microclimate, sheltered from the mistral
but perfectly placed to benefit from the summer breezes.
He will tell you every last detail about the house except
where it is. And finally, if that still doesn't convince you
that a rendezvous at his office is your first step to paradise,
he might, in desperation, agree to send you a dossier with
more photographs and a written description of this jewel
among houses.

Lesson number three: A coded vocabulary is used in
these descriptions which, after a few educational expeditions, you will learn to translate.

To start with, the price is often not specified, but indicated as being in one of three main categories:

1. *Prix intéressant,* the interesting price. This is
almost certainly not as low as you might expect from
the way it's described, but it's the best they can do if
you're determined to have something with a roof.

2. *Prix justifié,* the justified price. Well, it is an enormous amount of money. However, it does include a
marble bath and a fabulous twelfth-century dun-
geon, complete with the original manacles. Think of
the parties you could have.

3. *Prix: nous consulter,* the ultimate price. The sum being demanded is so outrageous that they hesitate to put it in writing. But if you come to the office and sit down, they will whisper a figure in your shocked and unbelieving ear.

To the base price, of course, must be added the costs of adapting the house to your personal requirements, and these costs will depend on the general state of repair and decoration. Here once again there are three main categories:

1. *Habitable.* You can in theory bring your suitcases and move right in, even though the plumbing and electrical wiring have seen better days—many of them—and there is a disturbing sag in the roofline. Nevertheless, you can live in it. The owners do.

2. *Restauré avec authenticité.* Old flagstones, exposed beams, curious crannies, and, often, a maze of small, somber rooms—all reflecting the way peasants used to live in the eighteenth century. Should you want more light and larger rooms, be prepared to rent a jackhammer and hire half a dozen masons.

3. *Restauré avec goût.* Taste is always difficult to define. Your idea of *bon goût*—or even *goût raffiné,* with all its swags and sconces and *trompe l'oeil* murals—is unlikely to be the same as that of the current owners. To an agent, though, all *goût* is considered *bon,* as it helps to establish a high price.

There are other code words which you'll pick up as you go along, but these should be enough to see you through your first afternoon. *Courage!* (And don't forget your checkbook.)

Pretending to Read

If there is a single Provençal tradition that every visitor should experience at least once, it is the siesta, taken externally.

Oddly enough, we have often found it very difficult to convince our guests that this is a healthy, sane, and refreshing way to spend a hot afternoon. They have arrived in Provence with their work ethics intact and their Anglo-Saxon distrust of self-indulgence poised to resist undisciplined, slightly decadent Mediterranean habits. Fear of inactivity comes bubbling to the surface. We haven't traveled all this way, they say, to do *nothing.*

I try to point out the mental and digestive benefits of doing nothing, but my advice falls on suspicious ears. The lunatic idea of an after-lunch game of tennis, however, is welcomed. Don't ask me why. I can only assume that the physical labor and potentially fatal strains on the heart involved in running after a ball in hundred-degree weather have some kind of perverse attraction. When reasoned argument fails to persuade the players of the risks they're taking, I'm obliged to call Monsieur Contini, our local Florence Nightingale. I ask him to come and park his ambulance next to the tennis court, and to leave the engine running. That will almost always bring the game to an end, and we are proud of the fact that we haven't lost any players yet. But there is still the problem of finding a civilized distraction for them that won't induce feelings of guilt and long faces around the dinner table.

The solution, we've discovered, is to give them a literary

excuse, an opportunity to add to their knowledge and enrich their minds by reading a book.

The choice of the book is all-important. Thrillers, adventure stories, and bodice-rippers won't do; they don't have enough weight, either mentally or physically. An improving tome is what's needed here, something that you've been meaning to read—something that you feel you *ought* to read—if only you could find the time. There are hundreds of suitable titles and authors, and we have a small selection of them, which is known as the Hammock Library. It includes Trollopes, Brontës, Austens, Hardys, Balzacs, Tolstoys, and Dostoevskys. But the book that has never failed—ever—in its appointed task is the three-volume boxed set of Edward Gibbon's *Decline and Fall of the Roman Empire*.

Tuck a volume under your arm and make your way through the trees to the shaded corner of the garden that overlooks the valley. Roll gently into the hammock, adjust the pillow, and let Gibbon come to rest on your stomach. Take in the sounds: The *cigales* are hard at it in the bushes, their tireless, scratchy, strangely soothing chirrup rising and falling in the warm afternoon air. Somewhere in the distance a dog barks—a half-hearted, heat-muffled bark that tails off into a falsetto yawn. Underneath the hammock, there is a hurried rustle in the dried grass as a lizard seizes a bug.

Supporting your elbows on the sides of the hammock, you lift Gibbon into the reading position. How heavy he is. Beyond the pages of the open book you see your toes, the rigging of the hammock, the motionless leaves of the scrub oak, and the long, blue panorama of the Luberon. A buzzard quarters the sky in lazy, graceful curves, its wings barely moving. Gibbon feels as though he's gained weight.

He declines and falls back to his resting place on your stomach and, as many have done before you in similar circumstances, you decide to allow yourself a brief doze, no longer than five minutes, before getting to grips with the Roman Empire.

Two hours later you wake up. The light on the mountain is beginning to change, a rim of sky above the crest turning from blue to violet. Gibbon is sprawled, pages akimbo, beneath the hammock where he fell. You dust him off, placing a bookmark at page 135 for the sake of appearances, before taking him back through the trees to the pool. A quick plunge is followed by the most wonderful sense of well-being, and you realize that a siesta isn't such a bad idea after all.

The Genetic Effects
of Two Thousand Years
# of Foie Gras

Old age is unlikely to be a keenly anticipated period in anybody's life, and no amount of euphemistic camouflage by the senior-citizen lobby can make it any more attractive than a long-awaited bill that finally arrives. Even so, it seems to me that growing old in Provence is not without its share of consolations. Some are mental, others are physical; one you can actually take to the bank.

Let us say you have retired, and that your main asset is your house. It suits you, and you have every intention of living in it until you make your final public appearance in the obituary columns. But the expenses of old age—and there's always something: the Ferrari for your grandson, the services of a live-in chef, the ruinous price of vintage wines—will inevitably increase every year, and there comes a moment when a windfall might be very welcome. This may be the appropriate time to consider selling your house under that particular French arrangement which is called *en viager.*

It's a gamble. You sell the house at a price below the full market value, but with yourself included as a fixture, having the right to continue in residence for the rest of your life. For you, it is like having your cake and living in it; for the buyer, it is a chance to acquire property at a discount—always providing that you, the ancient proprietor, have the good grace not to hang around for too long and make a lingering inconvenience of yourself. Some people find this system morbid. The French, always very practical in matters of money, see it as a chance for both buyer and seller to profit from natural causes.

But the gamble can sometimes backfire, as it did not long ago in the town of Arles, itself a monument to old age. Founded before Christ and noted for its pretty women, Arles was until 1997 the home of Madame Jeanne Calment. Her story is a testament to the bracing air of Provence and a warning to all property speculators.

She was born in 1875, and had met Van Gogh when she was a girl. At the age of 90, she decided to sell her apartment *en viager* to a local lawyer, a mere sprig in his forties, who had every reason to think he was making an impeccably sound investment.

But Calment lived on. And on. And on. She treated her skin with olive oil, ate almost a kilo of chocolate a week, rode a bicycle until she was 100, and gave up smoking when she was 117. According to official records, she was the oldest person in the world when she eventually died at the age of 122. As for the unfortunate lawyer, he had died the previous year, aged 77.

Calment, obviously, was an exception, one of those blips that spoil the symmetry of actuarial statistics. But while her accumulation of years was quite extraordinary, it would not surprise me if her record was eventually broken by one of the lively octogenarians I see every week—the antiques dealers who predate some of their stock, the elderly ladies who elbow you aside in the *épicerie* with the vigor of young girls, those gnarled but stately figures muttering words of encouragement to the tomatoes in their vegetable gardens. What is it about Provence that sustains them? What is their secret?

For several years, we lived near a family whose oldest member, known as Pépé, was a daily fascination to me. A small, lean man, invariably dressed in jacket and trousers of washed-out blue and a flat cap that never left his head, he would take his promenade along the road before coming up our drive to inspect the vines. He liked it best when there were people working in the long, green alleys— weeding, trimming overlong shoots, distributing the ration of sulfate—because then he could lean on his stick and supervise.

He was generous with his advice, which, as he often reminded his captive audience, was the result of more than eighty years' experience. If anyone had the impertinence and temerity to disagree with him on matters of wine or weather, he would reach back into his memory and produce some dusty scrap of evidence from the past to prove that he was right. "Of course," he once said, "you wouldn't remember the summer of 1947. Hailstones in

August, big as quails' eggs. The vines never recovered." That kind of remark was usually enough to put a stop to any loose talk about conditions being perfect for a vintage year. Optimism and nature don't mix, he used to say. After an hour or so, having satisfied himself that the vineyard was being properly attended to, he would walk back down our drive, along the road, and into his daughter-in-law's kitchen, no doubt to supervise the preparation of the midday meal.

I believe he was a contented man. The lines and wrinkles of his face went upward, as though a smile were on the way. (It often arrived, more gum than teeth, but no less delightful for that.) I never saw him agitated or upset. He was mildly critical of some modern novelties, such as noisy motorcycles, but delighted with others, particularly his large television set, which enabled him to indulge his weakness for old American soap operas. He died when he was ready, somewhere in his nineties, his passing marked by an affectionate village funeral.

There are others, plenty of others, like him. You see them moving, often quite briskly and always with great deliberation, to take up their seats in the café for a mid-morning nip of wine or pastis. You see them perched, like a row of amiable buzzards, on a wooden bench by the war memorial in the village *place,* their hands with swollen brown knuckles clasped over the tops of their sticks; or sitting on chairs in the shade outside their front doors, their eyes flickering up and down the street, missing nothing. By today's standards, they have had hard lives, working the land with little to show for their efforts but subsistence. No skiing trips, no winter breaks in the Caribbean, no golf, no tennis, no second homes, no new cars every three years, nothing of what is endlessly referred to as the good

life. But there they are, spry, happy, and apparently indestructible.

There are too many of them to be dismissed as exceptions, and whenever I see them I'm tempted to ask them to
explain their longevity. Nine times out of ten, the only
answer would be a shrug, and so I have been left to come
to my own unreliable conclusions.

Their generation seems to have escaped the modern
affliction of stress, which may be a result of having spent
their working lives coping with nature rather than with a
capricious boss. Not that nature—with its storms, forest
fires, and crop diseases—is either reliable or forgiving as
an employer. But at least it's free from personal malice and
the pressure of office politics, and it has no favorites. The
setback of a bad year is shared among neighbors, and
there's nothing to be done about it except hope for better
times to come. Working with (or fighting against) nature
teaches a man to be philosophical, and even allows him to
derive a certain perverse enjoyment from complaining.
Anyone who has lived among farmers will know the relish
with which they discuss misfortune, even their own.
They're as bad as insurance agents.

There must also be something reassuring about working
to the fixed and predictable rhythm of the seasons, knowing that spring and early summer and the harvest season
will be busy; knowing that winter will be slow and quiet. It
is a pattern of life that would probably drive most corpo-
rate executives—seething with impatience and ambition—into an early grave. But not all. I have a friend who,
like myself, is a refugee from the advertising business.
Some years ago, he moved to the Luberon, where he now
makes wine for a living. Instead of the big glossy car and
matching chauffeur, he drives to work on a tractor. His

problems are no longer with fractious clients but with the weather and the drifting bands of grape-pickers who come to the vineyards for the *vendange*. He has learned to do without what the French grandly call his entourage of secretaries and personal assistants. He has some difficulty remembering when he last wore a tie. He works long hours—longer than he ever used to in Paris—and makes less money. But he feels better, sleeps more soundly, and has a genuine pride in his work. Another contented man.

The day may come when he will want to join the ranks of what he calls the living antiques who spin out the days in the village café. In the meantime, he leads a life of sustained physical activity, and this must be an important ingredient in the recipe for ripe old age. The human body, so we are told by men of science (who spend most of their time sitting down), is a machine that thrives on use. When left idle, muscles atrophy, and other working parts of the system deteriorate more rapidly than they would if subjected to regular exercise. The urban solution is the jog and the gym. A more primitive alternative is the kind of manual labor that comes with country life, the rural aerobics necessary for existence. Bending and stretching to prune, lifting and piling sacks of fertilizer, cutting brush, clearing ditches, stacking logs—these are unglamorous chores, but wonderful exercise. A day of this produces an epic crop of blisters and excruciating stiffness. A month rewards you with a feeling of well-being and a distinct looseness of the waistband. A lifetime works wonders.

Even during the winter doldrums, the joys of hibernation will often be interrupted for exercise in the form of hunting. Now that game has become scarce in the Luberon, this is usually nothing more than a man taking his gun for a walk. But what a walk it is—steep and hard, a challenge for the legs, a flood of clean air for the lungs, a workout for the heart. And there seems to be no age limit for these armed optimists. I have occasionally come across hunters in the forest who look old enough to have preceded the invention of gunpowder. In a city, you might offer to help them cross the street. In the Luberon, they will walk you into the ground, chatting while you sweat to keep up with them.

The average age of cyclists, whom I always remembered as young men barely out of their teens, appears to have gone up, although the outfits remain misleadingly youthful. Brilliantly colored blurs, gleaming in skins of emerald green or purple Lycra, whir along the road like monstrous low-flying insects. It is not until they stop at the café for a beer that you see the grizzled heads and ropy veins of men who qualified for pensions years ago. Where does their energy come from? Don't they know they should be riddled with arthritis and tottering along to the pharmacy instead of knocking off a hundred kilometers before lunch? What are they taking?

What else but good food and a glass or two of wine? I once read a gloomy prescription written by the Greek physician Hippocrates: "Death sits in the bowels; a bad digestion is the root of all evil." If this is true, I have to assume that the long-lived Provençal bowel is a remarkably efficient item of equipment which, one can logically assume, is a direct result of what it has to deal with on a daily basis.

There are various worthy and quite appetizing theories to account for the healthy workings of the Provençal intestine. The regular consumption of olive oil is one, or frequent doses of garlic, helped down by red wine—anything from one to five glasses a day, depending on which scientific study you choose to believe. (Five glasses a day seems a good round number.) But I have yet to see any theory from learned nutritionists that explains my favorite statistic. The rate of heart disease among inhabitants of the southwestern part of France is lower than anywhere else in the country, which is frequently quoted as being lower than any other developed country except Japan.

And what do they exist on, these fortunate people of the southwest? Low-sodium gruel? Macrobiotic bean curd? Nut cutlets, with an occasional wicked glass of nonalcoholic, sugar-free sparkling-wine substitute? Alas for conventional dietary wisdom and the accepted rules of gastronomic prudence, a significant part of the southwestern diet is fat, particularly goose and duck fat. Potatoes are roasted in it, beans for the noble cassoulet are smothered in it, confits are preserved in it, and foie gras is goose fat gone to heaven. (Foie gras was actually invented by the Romans. The French, never slow to recognize a good thing when they eat it, gave it a French name and with their customary modesty have been claiming it as a national treasure ever since.) How is it possible that this rich and delicious regime can be part of a long and healthy life? Can we look forward to the day when foie gras will replace tofu and the soybean on nutritionally correct menus? Can it be that fat is actually good for you?

This might well depend on where the fat comes from, but the food police are not in the mood to make any trifling distinctions like that. For years, they have lectured us on the evils of fat; any kind of fat. I have even been told that in California, where one can marvel at people constructed of nothing but skin, bone, muscle, and health-giving amounts of silicone, authorities have seriously considered declaring fat a prohibited substance. Food products, even here in France, have to confess on their labels that they have committed a crime against the innards of society by including a percentage of fat. Fat has a terrible reputation. And so to find this corner of France thriving on massive amounts of something so sinful, so cholesterol-loaded and artery-threatening is, to say the least, mysterious.

Ever hopeful of discovering a link between foie gras and perfect health, I looked through several books on diet and nutrition, only to see the same old theories, variously disguised. But they were consistent about fat. It is a killer, so they all said, and if taken regularly will probably make you fall off your perch, clogged to death, in what should be the prime of your life. Looking for a second opinion, however unscientific, I decided to seek out a source closer to the grass roots of French nutrition. At first, I thought of consulting a chef, but the chefs whom I know and respect are more concerned with taste, which they consider to be their responsibility, rather than with the state of your heart, which is your affair. All I could hope for from them would be advice about which Sauternes go best with foie gras. What I needed was a more balanced view.

Monsieur Farigoule can rarely be accused of having a balanced view, but I went to see him anyway, hoping that he might have picked up some nutritional knowledge during his days as a schoolteacher. I found him defending the traditions of France in his usual spot at the bar, in his usual state of high indignation.

This time, the villain was a bottle of Chinese rosé that some mischievous friend had found in a local supermarket and given him, no doubt to get his blood pressure boiling.

He slid the bottle along the bar toward me, and I took a

look at the label: Great Wall Rosé Wine, produced by the Huaxia Winery in Hebei, China.

"First they try to inflict their truffles on us," he said. "And now *this*—this abomination in a bottle."

Abomination or not, I saw that the bottle was half empty. "What does it taste like?" I said.

He took a swig from his glass and chewed on it for a moment. "*Dégueulasse*—like a rice paddy strained through a sock. And not a very clean sock, either. As I said, an abomination. God knows why they allowed it into the country. Do we not make the best rosé wines in the world? The Tavel? The Bandol? The Ott? And what can we expect next? Chinese Calvados?"

With that, he climbed on his hobby horse and galloped off on a ten-minute rant about the evils of free trade, the threat to honest French wine-growers, and the horrendous possibilities that could easily follow now that the Chinese had their foot in the door. I tried once or twice to bring the conversation around to the benefits of a foie gras diet, but he wasn't having any of it. Chinese infiltration was the subject of the day, and for once the Americans were off the hook. However, it didn't get me any further in my research.

I didn't do much better with Régis, a normally reliable source of highly biased support for the French way of life. Of course foie gras was good for you, he said. Everybody knew that. And had I tasted the foie gras made by the Rivoire sisters in Gascony? *Une merveille.* But as far as solid medical evidence was concerned, Régis had nothing to offer.

In the end, I had to settle for Marius, the funeral connoisseur, who beckoned me into the café one morning. He obviously had some news, but before he could deliver himself of it I asked him if he had any theories about diet and longevity.

"You can eat what you like," he said, "but it doesn't make much difference. *La vieillesse nuit gravement à la santé.* Old age is hazardous to your health. No doubt about it."

At that, he brightened up, and leaned forward to give me the details of an interesting death that had just occurred. As usual when he discussed another man's plunge into eternity, he spoke in a low, serious voice. But it was clear that the story of *l'affaire Machin* gave him considerable enjoyment.

It seems that Monsieur Machin, now deceased, had been devoted throughout his adult life to the Loterie Nationale. Every week, hoping for fortune, he bought his ticket, which he tucked away for safekeeping in the top pocket of his only suit. The suit was locked in an armoire, and never saw the light of day except for rare brief outings at weddings and one memorable five-minute period when the President of France was driven slowly through the village. Once a week, the armoire was unlocked and the old unlucky ticket was replaced in the suit pocket by a new one. This had been Machin's habit for thirty years—thirty years during which he had never won even a centime.

The end came suddenly for Machin, in the full heat of summer, and he was buried in the correct manner befitting his status in the community. (He had served for many years in the local post office.) The following week, such is the unfairness of life, it was discovered that his final lottery ticket was a winner—not of multimillions, but of a substantial sum that ran into several hundred thousand francs.

Marius paused to allow the injustice of it all to sink in,

and to feign surprise at his empty glass. Before continuing, he peered around the café, as though making sure that what he was about to say remained confidential. There was, he said, *un petit problème*. Machin had been buried in his one and only suit, as was right and proper. In the top pocket of the suit was the winning ticket, just two meters underground. And the lottery rules were very strict: No ticket, no money. To dig up the body, to defile a grave, was unthinkable. To leave it would be to lose a small fortune.

"C'est drôle, n'est-ce pas?" Marius nodded and grinned, a man with an infinite capacity for being amused at the vagaries of fate—always providing they affected someone else.

"Not so funny for the family," I said.

"Ah, you wait." He tapped the side of his nose. "The story isn't over yet. Too many people know."

I had awful visions of grave robbers creeping at night through the village cemetery, the scuffle of shovels in the earth, the sudden sharp creak of wood as the coffin was forced open, the grunt of satisfaction as the precious ticket was retrieved. But surely, I said to Marius, there was some way the family could claim the prize without disturbing the corpse.

He wagged the inevitable index finger at me, as though I'd suggested something ridiculous and impossible. Rules were rules, he said. Make an exception here, and it would open the door to all kinds of bogus stories about disappearing tickets—eaten by the dog, blown away by the mistral, washed into oblivion by the laundry—there would be no end to it. Marius shook his head, and then, remembering something, reached into a pocket of his army surplus jacket.

"I have an idea that we could work on together," he said, taking out a rolled-up magazine and smoothing the crumpled pages. "Take a look at that."

It was a copy of *Allo!* magazine, the chronicle of minor celebrities that is an item of standard equipment in hairdressing salons and dentists' waiting rooms. Colored pictures of the rich and royal at play, at home, and, occasionally, at funerals. That's what had prompted the idea.

"You once worked in advertising," said Marius. "You will see the possibilities."

He had thought it all through. His scheme was to bring out a companion magazine devoted to prominent, recently dead figures. It would be called *Adieu* in France, or *Goodbye* for the Anglo-Saxons. The editorial content would be obituaries lifted from newspapers, illustrated with photographs taken during the lifetime of the chosen subjects—"Seen here in happier times," as Marius said. There would be a regular special feature, Funeral of the Month, and advertising support would be provided by funeral homes, wreath makers, florists, coffin manufacturers, and—most important—catering services, a well-fed wake being an essential part of any self-respecting funeral.

"Well?" said Marius. "*C'est pas con, eh?* It would be a gold mine. Somebody famous dies every week." He leaned back, eyebrows raised, and we sat in silence for a few moments, contemplating death and money.

"You're not serious," I said.

"Of course I'm serious. Everybody thinks about it. You, for instance," he said, "you must have thought about how you would like to die."

My hopes for an acceptable death could be summed up in one word: sudden. But this wasn't good enough for

Marius. The old vulture was interested in the details, the where and how, and when I couldn't provide them, he shook his head in disapproval. One of the very few certainties in life, and I had given it less thought than what I was going to have for dinner. He, on the other hand, had made his plans; a perfect scheme, the final triumph, a mingling of pleasures that anyone fortunate enough to be present would never forget. In his enthusiasm, he might have been describing a treat that he had been looking forward to for years—which, if all went according to his expectations, it would be.

The first essential was a beautiful summer day, a sky fading from deep to paler blue in the heat of high noon, a light breeze, the rustling chirrup from a choir of *cigales* providing background music in the bushes. Death in the rain, so Marius said, would spoil an otherwise agreeable occasion. The second essential was a good appetite, because Marius had decided that his final moments on earth should be spent having lunch on the shaded terrace of a restaurant.

A three-star restaurant, naturally, and one with a cellar containing wines of unimaginable elegance and expense: golden-white Burgundies, first-growth Bordeaux, late-nineteenth-century Yquem, vintage champagnes from the oldest vines. These would be chosen, with no regard for price, several days before the lunch. This would allow the chef time to create a suitably exquisite meal to accompany the wines. Marius picked up his glass of the café's ten-franc *rouge ordinaire*, took a sip, shrugged at the taste, and continued.

Congenial company was also important on this special day, and Marius had already picked out an appropriate guest—Bernard, a friend of many years. Not only a friend, but a local legend, notorious for his reluctance to dip into his pocket for fear of disturbing his money, a man who had made an art of frugality. In all the time that they had known each other, Marius could only remember two occasions when Bernard had paid his way in the café, and then only because the *toilettes* had been occupied, cutting off his usual escape route at the time of reckoning. But he was a good companion, full of stories, and the two men would have hours of memories to share over the food and wine.

As for the meal—the *menu de mort*—Marius was still refining the exact procession of dishes. There might be a few deep-fried *courgette* flowers to alert the palate. Some foie gras, of course. Maybe a charlotte of Sisteron lamb with eggplant, or pigeon in spiced honey, or pork slowly cooked with sage (Marius was quite happy to leave the choice to the chef), and then roasted goat cheese with rosemary, followed by a custard and cherry tart, or a fresh peach and *verveine* soup. . . .

He stopped, his eyes looking past me toward this future banquet, and I wondered how he was going to find the time or the inclination to die when there was so much on the table demanding his attention. A brief shake of his head brought his thoughts back to the climax of lunch.

"This is how it will pass," he said. "We have eaten the meal of a lifetime, we have drunk like kings, we have laughed and exchanged stories, lied about our successes with women, vowed eternal friendship, drained the last wonderful bottle. And yet the afternoon is still young. We are not quite ready to leave. Another glass or two to settle the stomach, and what could be better than a cognac made in 1934, the year of my birth? I raise my hand to summon the waiter—and then, *paf!*"

The Genetic Effects of 2,000 Years of Foie Gras

"Paf?"

"A *crise cardiaque,* a fatal heart attack." Marius slumped forward on the table, turning his head to look up at me. "I die instantly, but I have a smile on my face." He winked. "Because Bernard gets the bill."

He sat back in his chair and crossed himself. "Now *that's* a death."

Later that day, I took the dogs for a walk on the plateau of the Claparèdes above Bonnieux. It was early evening, and over the mountains to the east a three-quarter moon was rising, pale and milky against the blue sky, balanced by the sun falling in the west. The air was warm and dry, sharp with the scent of the *sariette* that grows wild in pockets of earth between the rocks. The only sound was the wind, the only visible souvenir of man's presence a few meters of collapsed stone wall slumped among the bushes. The view could hardly have changed in hundreds of years, perhaps thousands, and it was a reminder of the quick blink of time that represents a human life.

I thought of Madame Calment's one hundred twenty-two years, fueled by chocolate and cigarettes, and of the nostrums that various Provençal experts had recommended to me for a long and healthy existence. Cloves of raw garlic, a daily teaspoon of cayenne pepper taken in a glass of water, *tisanes* of lavender, the soothing lubricant of olive oil. None of my experts had mentioned foie gras, which was a disappointment; but then, neither had they spoken of an even more essential ingredient, *joie de vivre*—the ability to take pleasure from the simple fact of being alive.

You can see and hear this expressed in a dozen small

ways: the gusto of a game of cards in a café, the noisy, good-humored exchanges in the market, the sound of laughter at a village fête, the hum of anticipation in a restaurant at the start of Sunday lunch. If there is such a thing as a formula for a long and happy old age, perhaps it's no more than that—to eat, to drink, and to be merry. Above all, to be merry.

Discovering Oil

I was born in England during the dark ages of gastronomy, a time when most good things to eat were either unavailable or rationed. Butter and meat were measured out in ounces, once a week if we were lucky. A fresh egg was an infrequent treat. Potatoes came in the form of powder—I seem to remember it was called POM—to be mixed with water and turned into a tepid, off-white sludge. Presented with my first postwar banana, at the age of six, I had no idea how to unwrap it. Chocolate was an unimaginable luxury. Olive oil didn't exist.

It eventually made its appearance in England, only to be regarded as a curiosity coming from the wrong side of the Channel, and definitely unsuitable for consumption with fish and chips or roast beef and Yorkshire pudding. If you were an adventurous cook who felt the need to buy some of this suspect foreign fluid, the only place you could have any hope of finding it was in the chain of pharmacies known as Boots the Chemist. Here, next to the cough remedies, bunion cures, denture cleaners, chest rubs, and dandruff shampoos, you might be lucky enough to come across a small, plain bottle of medicinal appearance labeled Olive Oil. It was not considered necessary to put any details on the label—not the country of origin, not the grower's name, not the mill where the oil had been pressed, and certainly nothing as inflammatory to the English imagination as extra virgin. Olive oil was merely a commodity; not even a popular commodity.

Today, after more than two thousand years of being more or less confined to southern Europe, olive oil has spread north to those cold, gray countries where olive trees very sensibly refuse to grow. It has spread west across the Atlantic, too, although the early pioneer olives suffered a very discouraging start on arrival in America, being plunged into glasses of icy gin to shiver in the depths of a Martini.

Luckily for all of us, the world is now a more civilized place. You can still find olives behind the bar, but the oil has been promoted—first to the kitchen, and more recently to the tables in desperately fashionable restaurants of the kind that present you with a separate list of mineral waters. In these often highly self-conscious establishments, the chefs make a point of mentioning their chosen oil by name, and extra virgin has become the heroine of many a house salad dressing. Slugs of hard liquor before dinner are out. Saucers of oil are in, to be mopped up with bread. Alas, it can only be a matter of time before oil snobs start sending back the original saucer of Tuscan *frantoio* and demanding the less well known—and therefore more highly prized by status eaters—*corni cabra* from Toledo.

This increasingly widespread flow of oil is encouraging news for your heart and your arteries, as well as your taste buds. Doctors agree, as much as doctors ever agree about anything, that olive oil is good for you. It helps the digestion, fights bad cholesterol, slows down the aging process of skin, bones, and joints, and is even said to protect against certain forms of cancer. In other words, it can be enjoyed without guilt or digestive remorse, and world consumption is on the rise.

But among oil men here in Provence there is a mild irritation, an occasional touch of gastronomic pique, that the best olive oil is almost always associated with Italy. Given the facts, this is hardly surprising. Italy produces 25 percent of the oil coming from the countries around the Mediterranean, and for years the Italian growers—"those Tuscan windbags," as Régis calls them—have been marketing it with imagination and great success. In contrast, Provence accounts for no more than three percent of the Mediterranean total, and so far has been uncharacteristically modest about its efforts.

I came across these production figures in the course of pursuing an ambition I have had for years. One morning long ago, when I saw that first sunny slope planted with olive trees, I thought what a delight it would be to have a grove—even a tiny, amateur-sized grove—to call my own and be able to look at every day. I loved the prehistoric appearance of the trunks, the generous spread of branches, and the way the leaves changed color in the wind from green to silver-gray as they rippled in the air.

But taking pleasure in the tree's appearance was just the start. Over the years I have developed an addict's taste for olives; on their own, or as black, creamy *tapenade* spread over quails' eggs, in tarts and salads, in *daubes,* or studded into loaves of bread. And then there is the oil. We cook with it, lace our soups with it, preserve goat cheeses in it, and now I've taken to drinking a small glass of it every day before breakfast. It is one of the oldest, purest tastes in the world, a taste that hasn't changed for thousands of years.

The thought of having all the joys of the olive available just steps away in the field behind the house was so exciting that I managed to overlook an obvious problem: The trees that I admired and coveted, those gnarly, wrinkled, timeless monuments to nature, were each at least a hundred years old. If I planted young trees—a collection of five-year-olds, let's say, very little more than shoots—I would have to add an extra century to my life to be sure of enjoying the results. I like to think that I'm an optimist, but there are limits.

It was Régis who attempted to put me straight, as he so often does. If I wanted venerable trees—anything from one hundred to three hundred years old—he knew a man from Beaumes-de-Venise who could help. There is a microclimate near Beaumes-de-Venise, a pocket of land where olive trees grow thick on the hills, and Régis's friend would be delighted to dig up some prime old specimens for me. Just two minor conditions, Régis said, would have to be observed: Payment would have to be in cash, and delivery of the trees would need to be made at night.

"Why is that?" I asked. "Aren't the trees his?"

Régis spread both hands, palms down, in front of him, and waggled them as if he were trying to keep his balance.

"Not exactly," he said. "But they will be. He'll inherit them from his father."

"But his father has to die first."

"*Tout à fait*," said Régis. "That's why they have to be moved at night, so the neighbors don't see anything. The old boy won't know. He never goes out."

Somehow I didn't find the idea of an illicit olive grove very appealing, and so I asked Régis if he knew of a more respectable tree dealer.

"Well, they exist," he said. "But you have to be careful. They import the trees." He raised his eyebrows and shook his head. "You wouldn't want *Italian* trees, would you?" From the tone of his voice, it sounded as though they suffered from some incurable disease. But of course they weren't French, and this, as far as Régis was concerned, disqualified them from any serious consideration.

In fact, he made me realize that I wasn't at all sure what I wanted. Old trees, certainly. Beautiful trees. But what kind of trees? I'd read enough to know that there were at least a dozen different varieties growing in Provence, some smaller than others, some more resistant to extreme cold and the unwelcome attentions of the olive fly, some that gave a bigger crop—useful as general background information, but lacking in the kind of detail necessary for a potential grove-owner. What I needed was someone who could tell a confused novice whether to plant *salonenque, picholine,* or *aglandau,* when and where to plant, how to fertilize and prune. What I needed was a professor of olives.

Experts are not difficult to find in Provence. All the bars I know are full of them, but the trick is to meet an expert whose knowledge is equal to his enthusiasm. This time, I

was lucky. A friend knew of a man—*un homme sérieux*—
who had a small but growing business devoted to olive oil,
and not just the oil of his native Haute Provence. He had
started to do for olive oil what *négociants* have traditionally done for wine: finding the best from the hundreds of
growers and thousands of groves scattered around the
Mediterranean basin. That was his patch, and it included
Andalusia, Catalonia, Crete, Galilee, Greece, Sardinia,
Tuscany, the Atlas mountains—wherever good oil was
made. His name, appropriately enough, was Olivier, his
company was called Oliviers & Co., and his head office
was in the village of Mane, not far from Forcalquier.

It's a small village, and a modest head office—an old
stone house, plain and substantial. The offices are
upstairs, and on the ground floor is a shop where the visitor can browse among an international selection of oils.
Not only browse, but sample; bottles and stubby porcelain
tasting spoons are laid out on the table so that you can sip
before you buy. You can compare, for instance, an oil from
Andalusia with one from Chianti, or another from the valley of Les Baux—first-pressing extra virgins, all of them,
each made from a different type of olive, each with its own
highly distinctive bouquet and flavor, and each with its
own particular color, a range of delicate shades from jade
green to a fine transparent gold. Olive oils, as I discovered
during my first half hour, can vary in character as much as
wine. Even my palate, a sadly abused organ that morning
after too many jolts of turbo-charged coffee, could distin-
guish between them.

The similarities with wine were emphasized by the tasting notes for each oil. These were written in language that
had echoes of the *cave:* hints of citrus and blackcurrant

buds, of artichokes and pepper, of fresh herbs—words and phrases that you might hear bandied about by those grand old men with florid noses who hold court in the cellars of Châteauneuf-du-Pape. The one major difference is that there's no point in laying down a few cases of oil for your self-indulgent old age. Unlike many wines, oil doesn't improve with the years; young is best.

With my palate now well lubricated and my teeth still slick with oil, I went upstairs to meet Olivier. Dark, short-haired, and bespectacled, he has a quiet and academic air about him, and a scholarly vocabulary to go with it, as I found when I asked him to explain a phrase that had puzzled me ever since I first saw it displayed on a bottle of oil from Lucca, in Italy. *Extra vérgine.*

I could never understand how anything could be extra virgin. This has always seemed to me like describing a woman as extra pregnant. How can there be degrees of virginity? I'd assumed it to be one of those flights of Italian self-promotion—my virgin is better than your virgin—that served no purpose other than to look impressive on a label.

Olivier looked at me over the top of his glasses. "In fact," he said, "there are three stages of virginity. All olive oil contains free fatty acids. To be described as extra virgin, an oil must contain less than one percent of these acids. More than one percent but less than one and a half, and you have a *vierge fine.* Anything above this, up to 3.3 percent, can only qualify as virgin." He smiled. "Virgin *ordinaire.* You understand?"

He went on to talk about vintages of olive oil, the aging process that oils go through from the moment of pressing (extra virgin keeps longer than the lesser virgins, I was pleased to hear), and we were just getting into the deeper waters of organoleptic traits—taste factors, to you and me—when Olivier looked at his watch and said it was time to go.

As we drove to Forcalquier for that most essential part of the Gallic learning process, a long and well-considered lunch, the lesson continued. I was already aware that olive oil is good for you in a general sense, but I had no idea of some of the more refined applications. For example, oil beaten up with an egg yolk makes a face mask guaranteed to nourish the driest complexion. Oil laced with essence of rosemary takes the soreness out of stiff and aching muscles. A mixture of oil and green mint rubbed on to the temples is said to do wonders for migraine sufferers. For those about to suffer—from having too much to eat and drink—a tablespoon of oil taken neat before the start of any wretched excess coats the stomach lining, tempers the hangover, and assures a smooth and well-ordered *transit intestinal*. Relief is also promised from constipation, as well as from that particularly French national ailment, the *crise de foie* (a rebellion of the liver following a surfeit of rich food and an ill-advised second bottle of heavy wine). And so, since it keeps your innards in such prime working order, it follows that generous daily doses of extra virgin help you live longer. All in all, Olivier managed to make olive oil seem like a panacea for everything that ails man short of a broken leg.

Perhaps some of these are exaggerated claims, but I was happy to believe them. There are so many things in life I enjoy, from sun to cigars, which I'm told are bad for me that a healthy pleasure is a rare treat. Anyway, I wasn't about to argue as we arrived in Forcalquier and made our way across the main square to the restaurant with a curious name—Le Lapin Tant Pis—and a chef, Gérard Vives, whom I wish I had as a neighbor. The chef was joining us for lunch, always a reassuring sign, and so were two of Olivier's colleagues. Not for the first time, I found myself an ignoramus among experts.

Olivier produced a bottle of his latest discovery, a local oil from Les Mées, and this we had to taste before lunch started in earnest. I was half expecting porcelain tasting spoons to be whipped out of pockets, but the technique here was a little more rustic. Bread was distributed, that irresistible, resilient bread which gives under a gentle squeeze from the fingers. Pieces were torn from the loaf, and I watched the professionals on either side of me using their thumbs to make small indentations in their bread. The bottle was passed, and the indentations were filled with oil. Heads were lowered, and noses were applied to take in the bouquet. Then, with restrained, birdlike sips, the oil was tasted, held in the mouth and swirled around the back teeth before being swallowed. Then we ate the bread, licked our thumbs, and had some more.

This is only one of several tasting methods, and simpler than most. In Corsica, for instance, they put a few drops of oil into the hand, and warm them with a finger. Whether you then lick the hand or the finger depends, so I'm told, on the Corsican. Or there's the potato method, in which oil is drizzled on to pieces of steamed potato, with a mouthful of apple eaten in between tasting to clear the palate. In every case, a few deep breaths are recommended to mix air with the oil in your mouth, which releases all those organoleptic traits. This sounds easy enough until you try it. You discover, quickly and embarrassingly, that some practice is required before you master the knack of holding the oil in your half-open mouth without dribbling. When tasters are gathered together, you can always tell a beginner by his oily chin; in this case, mine.

But at least I was able to keep enough in my mouth to appreciate it; a lovely oil, spicy, with a very faint nip of peppery bitterness at the end. Olivier told me it had been pressed from three different varieties—*aglandau*, *picholine*, and *bouteillan*—all of them resistant to the olive fly and hardy enough to survive the often severe Haute Provence winter. The kind of olives, perhaps, that I should think of planting.

One thing led to another, as it often does during a fine four-course lunch, and by the time we had finished I'd been invited to meet the trees that had produced the oil. The time of the harvest would be best, so Olivier said, around St. Catherine's Day at the end of November. He could even arrange a guide—a man of passion and *grande valeur*—to instruct me as he took me through the groves.

I met Jean-Marie Baldassari at his office in Oraison, an instantly likeable man—friendly, relaxed, and with an air of calm that I've noticed before in people who work with nature and the seasons. He runs the local oil syndicate, and it soon became clear that the love of his professional life was the olive. A tree of great intelligence, he called it, a camel among trees, able to store enough water to keep it going through long periods of drought, an almost everlasting tree. There were some around Jerusalem, he told me, that are estimated to be two thousand years old.

In Provence, the olive has gone through some hard times, suffering from both man and nature: from freak frosts like the memorably brutal year of 1956, or from a long-lasting tendency among farmers to replace olive groves with more profitable vineyards. (Since 1929, the number of olive trees in Provence has declined from eight million to two million.) And then there's general neglect. You see the victims on deserted, overgrown hillsides, their trunks strangled by ropes of wild ivy, entire trees almost hidden by brambles, apparently smothered to death. Amazingly, they survive. Cut away the ivy and the brambles, clean up the area around the base of the trunk, prune the tangle of branches, and in a year or so there will be olives. The intelligent camel, so it seems, is practically indestructible, capable of springing back to life again after going through an arboreal nightmare. I could see why Jean-Marie had such an admiration for it.

But even if every neglected tree in Provence were to be restored to perfect health, the production of oil would still be tiny compared to Italy and Spain (which I later heard described as "the Kuwait of olive oil"). Provence can't attempt to compete on quantity. It has to be quality, and as with almost everything in France that is particularly good to eat or drink, this means a highly prized classification— A.O.C., or *appellation d'origine controlée.*

An A.O.C. is similar to a manufacturer's guarantee, with the important difference that the manufacturers can't award it to themselves. It has to be officially sanctioned: Tests have to be conducted, production conditions scrutinized, reams of paperwork completed, and, of course, tastings organized. I like to think that working for the A.O.C. people is almost as well-fed an occupation as being a Michelin inspector. The rules are strict, whether the *appellation* is given to wine, cheese, or chickens. These have to come from the stated area (the *origine*), and the quality has to be of a sufficiently high standard to deserve the distinction. It's a system that encourages excellence, protects against imitations, and lets customers know exactly what they can expect to get for their money. Two Provençal oils, from Nyons and Les Baux, already have A.O.C. status, and the oils of Haute Provence will have joined them by the end of 1999.

"*Bon*," said Jean-Marie. "So much for facts and figures. I expect you'd like to see some oil."

There are seven working mills in Haute Provence, and our first stop was the Moulin des Pénitents outside Les Mées. Driving north along straight, empty roads, we were heading toward the Montagne de Lure, with its winter cap of snow. The day was bright and hard, and I didn't envy the olive-pickers who had been out there on the hills since early morning. To make a single liter of oil takes five kilos, or more than ten pounds, of olives, and no machine yet invented can pick the fruit without damaging the tree. Olives must be harvested by hand. I wondered how long the fingers would last before they froze. As Jean-Marie said, you have to love the trees to do the work.

The shock for a newly picked olive, after a brief lifetime of peace and quiet, must be considerable. It might have been tenderly plucked from the tree, but conditions go rapidly downhill from there: tossed into a sack, bundled into a van, and delivered into the cacophony of a mechanical torture chamber. First to be washed, then to be crushed, then to be pressed, finally to be whirled around in a centrifuge.

For humans, the level of noise in an oil mill means that all communication must be carried out in a bellow delivered no more than six inches from the ear, which was a slight obstacle to my education. Even so, Jean-Marie was able to penetrate the racket and guide me from the start of the process to the finish, from the sacks of olives waiting their turn in the washing machine at one end to the greeny-gold flow of oil pouring out at the other. There was a wonderful smell in the air, rich and slippery and promising, a warm smell I always associate with sunshine.

We watched as the olives, stripped of twigs and leaves, washed and shining, went through to the next stage, the *broyage*, which crushes them into a dense, dark paste. "You're probably wondering about the pits," said Jean-Marie.

Ah, the pits. It turns out that they are more useful and important than anyone might think. At one time, there was a feeling among certain avant-garde olive-men that the quality of their oil would be improved by extracting the pits and pressing only the flesh, an extra complication and expense. But they discovered that oil processed in this way didn't keep. There is a natural preservative contained in the pits, and without that the oil quickly turns rancid. It doesn't pay to tamper with nature, Jean-Marie said. God knows best.

With our eardrums still vibrating from the noise of the machinery, we went through to the front office of the mill, where two growers were leaning against the counter. One of them, ruddy-faced and jolly, had retired, but had dropped in to see how the harvest was going.

"*Alors*," he said to the other grower, "*ça coule?*"

From what I had seen next door, the oil was flowing like a young torrent, but it was obviously not correct form to admit it. The other grower frowned and wagged his hand, a tentative admission that things could be worse. "*Eh,*" he said. "*Quelques gouttes.*" A few drops.

The woman behind the counter was smiling, and when I asked her if the crop was good this year, she nodded, pointing to a tall glass flask. It was filled with a sample of early season oil, undiluted *aglandau*. When I held it up to the sunlight the oil was so thick it looked almost solid. "That's Monsieur Pinatel's oil," she said. "We keep all the batches separate. I could tell you where each oil comes from—not the tree, but probably the field. Like wine."

It was time to move on. Jean-Marie—perhaps the only living Frenchman who works during lunch—had olive business to attend to, and we agreed to meet in the early afternoon for a conducted tour of the trees. I was to wait for him in the café at Dabisse, the Bar Moderne.

Country bars tend to reflect the character of the country, and the bare, hard surfaces of the Bar Moderne had some of the austerity of a windy Haute Provence hilltop. Gusts of cold air came through the door with every customer, to be replaced by gusts of hot air as greetings were exchanged and conversations started up. Men who spend their working lives outdoors, where speech has to compete with distance and the clatter of tractors, seem to develop amplified voices. They boom at each other, and their laughter has the resonance of minor explosions.

There was an interesting selection of headwear on display that day, modeled by representatives of three different generations. The oldest man in the room, huddled over a pastis in the corner, his hand curved protectively around his glass, was wearing something that might have belonged to a Russian tank commander in World War II— a canvas creation in olive drab with long flaps that hung down like a hound's ears on either side of his raw, white-stubbled face. His younger companions had either flat caps or woolen bonnets; one had both, the cap jammed down over the bonnet. Only the young man behind the bar, with his baseball cap, had made any concessions to modern fashion.

Discovering Oil

On the screen of the television set cantilevered out from the back wall, inhabitants of another planet were mouthing and capering in a series of music videos, unwatched by the clientele. A dog made the rounds of the tables, prospecting for sugar lumps. I drank a glass of chilly red wine and looked through the window at a suddenly darker sky. The sun had gone. A bank of heavy clouds the color of pewter had moved in with the wind, and it was going to be bitter on the hills.

I was delivered into the care of Monsieur Pinatel, who was standing at the entrance of an old stone barn, sniffing the air. After a leathery handshake, we got into his van, taking a narrow dirt track that led past a curiously decorative apple orchard. Rows of trees, gaunt and leafless, each connected to the next by drooping swags of fine-mesh netting. From a distance, it looked as though someone had started to gift wrap the entire orchard but had lost interest before adding the final ornamental touches. "It's to protect the fruit when there's a hailstorm," said Monsieur Pinatel. "Without the netting, they won't insure the crop." He grunted and shook his head. "Insurance. Thank God we don't have to do the same for the olives."

I saw what he meant as we left the orchard behind us and entered an ocean of olive trees. Thousands of them stretched across the hillside, looking like primitive, leafy sculptures against the bare stony ground. Most of them had been there for two hundred years; the veterans were twice that age. The crop ran into many hundreds of thousands of olives, and each one had to be taken from the branches by hand.

We stopped at the end of a long avenue of trees where the pickers were at work—men and women from the surrounding villages, doing what their great-great-grandparents had done before them. In those days, when travel was by mule or foot, the olive harvest used to be one of the few times in the year when inhabitants of isolated villages had a practical excuse to get together. This was a rare chance for young men to meet young women, and romantic attachments were often formed under the trees. A sackful of olives must have had the same allure as a bouquet of red roses. Love blossomed, and marriages were arranged. The first male child was often named Olivier.

Customs may have changed, and so have the pickers' tools, but the technique of picking is much the same as it was two thousand years ago. The *bache,* a giant plastic sheet, is placed on the ground around the base of the tree to catch the olives. These are taken from the branches with a tool that you can imagine being used to groom a very large shaggy animal—a short-handled comb, perhaps eight inches wide, with a row of blunt teeth. When the lower branches have been combed clean, the picker reaches the upper parts of the tree by climbing a triangular ladder, broad at the bottom, narrow at the top. Once up the ladder, half the picker's body disappears; all you can see are pairs of legs sprouting from the foliage, bizarre growths, most of them covered in denim. Above the sound of the wind, I could hear the steady, soft plop of olives falling on to the *bache* and the occasional curse as a twig whipped back to sting a frozen cheek. It was slow, cold work.

Driving home at the end of the day, my hands and feet thawing out in the warmth of the car, it was easy to understand what had made so many farmers give up the olive in favor of the grape. A vineyard will give you a quicker return on your investment; after three years or so, you're in business, and working conditions are more congenial.

Apart from pruning, most of the hard labor is done when you can feel the sun on your shoulders, which is easier on the bones as well as the disposition. And, if the wine is good enough, grapes can make a handsome living for the men who grow them. Olives are different. I heard it again and again: Nobody gets rich from growing olives.

I realized that my own affection for olives was based on emotion rather than practicality. I was drawn to the history of the trees, their stubborn resistance to natural disasters, and their refusal to die. I would never tire of looking at the shimmer of their leaves in the sun and the muscles of their massive trunks, swollen and twisted with the effort of writhing up from the earth. These feelings, so I had always thought, were typical of an amateur attracted to the picturesque. It was a surprise and a great pleasure to find that they were shared by the hard-headed farmers out on those cold hills. You have to love the trees to do the work.

Friday Morning
in Carpentras

You will often see, on your travels around the Vaucluse, small fields planted with a few straggly rows of infant oak trees and guarded by severe black and yellow notices. *Défense de pénétrer sous peine de sanctions correctionelles graves*, they say, and draw the reader's attention to articles 388 and 444 in the French penal code. I have no idea what the punishments might be. A manacled trip to Devil's Island, possibly, or prodigious fines and confinement in a health spa. One shudders at the ghastly possibilities.

Although I take these warnings seriously, it's clear that others don't; the notices are routinely stolen, defaced, or used for target practice by hunters. But in theory you could be prosecuted for ignoring them and venturing into the field. It is—or will be, if God, the weather, and the vagaries of soil and spores permit—a precious field, a field where wealth lies just a few centimeters beneath the surface. A truffle field.

Not long ago, we had the good luck to spend some time in a house on the edge of the grandfather of all truffle fields; an entire estate, in fact, an area of more than a hundred acres. It was by far the most impressive example I have ever seen of man's determination to cultivate the ferociously expensive and notoriously capricious black truffle—the "divine tubercule" that makes gourmets quiver in anticipation even as they reach for their wallets.

We became friendly with the owners, Mathilde and Bernard, who told us some of the history of the estate. It had been rough grazing land when Bernard's father saw its potential and bought it many years ago, but he was a man with a patient eye on the future. He was prepared to wait for his truffles. He must also have been an optimist, because black truffles have minds of their own and tend to grow where they want to rather than where they're supposed to. All one can do is help to create the right conditions, keep the fingers firmly crossed, and wait for five, ten, or fifteen years.

This was done. Twenty-five thousand truffle oaks were planted on well-drained, sloping ground, and several kilometers of irrigation pipes laid down. An impressive investment, everyone agreed, although the irrigation system was the cause of great amusement to the locals at the time. Who had ever heard of watering truffle oaks as if they were geraniums? It was money thrown away. He'd be sorry.

But Bernard's father had made a very thorough study of the care and feeding of truffle oaks, and knew that the trees needed refreshment during the heat of the summer. He wanted to leave as little as possible to chance and nature, and had laid down irrigation as an insurance against drought. In unusually dry years, when the August storms didn't arrive as they should, his trees still had water. In the winters that followed the droughts, when others were scratching the earth and finding nothing, he had truffles. The locals stopped laughing. And, paying him a kind of backhanded compliment, some of them started poaching.

The problems of protecting a large, remote tract of land from stealthy invasion are considerable. They were made even more difficult in this case because truffle poachers usually work at night. Their dogs, trained to the scent, don't have to see; their noses take them where they need to go. Working in the dark, the poacher's traditional excuse if stopped and questioned—"I was just taking Fido for a walk"—is less than convincing. Two in the morning is an odd hour for a stroll. But then, working in the dark, the poacher is very rarely caught. Sometimes he is heard, occasionally glimpsed, seldom nailed. What can one do?

All kinds of discouragements were tried. Notices threatening prosecution and fines proved useless; a succession of night watchmen found it impossible to cover such an expanse of country. Geese were recruited as a mobile alarm system, but found to be messy and ineffective. (Some of them didn't live long either, being easy to kill and rather good to eat.) Following the goose experiment, head-high wire fences were erected. The poachers promptly bought wire-cutters.

Finally, a team of four guard dogs—big beasts, the size of German shepherds and very fast—came to live and work on the property. Confined to their kennels during the day, they are let out at night and given the run of the land. They have been trained not to attack the poacher, but to concentrate their attentions on his dog, and the system works. Presented with the choice of retreat or death, the poacher's dog suddenly remembers an urgent appointment elsewhere, and off he goes. Without the dog's powers of detection to guide him, the poacher is finished. He can dig all night without finding anything more than handfuls of dirt. He might as well go home.

A good truffle dog is money in the bank, as we saw one afternoon at the beginning of the season. She was a gray-haired, whiskery mongrel, low to the ground as many of the best truffle dogs are, and completely absorbed in her work. We followed her as she went slowly through the trees, head down, nose cocked, tail wagging. From time to time she would stop and scratch, surprisingly gently, at the earth, and she never failed. There was always a truffle just below the surface, to be eased out with a U-shaped pick while she nosed at her master's pocket for her reward, a tiny piece of Gruyère.

The truffle season extends roughly from the first frost to the last, and during much of that time the kitchen of Mathilde and Bernard's farmhouse takes on a pleasantly perfumed air. The scent of truffles, ripe and powerful, greets you as you go through the door, and you may be fortunate enough to be offered one of the specialties of the house. This is the Rolls Royce of butters: alternate layers of butter and thinly sliced fresh truffles, spread on toast, sprinkled with grains of *gros sel*, the coarse gray sea salt, and accompanied by a glass or two of red wine. If that doesn't set you up for lunch, nothing will.

Toward the end of each week during the season, you might see in the corner of the kitchen a couple of capacious straw baskets, their contents covered with a damp linen cloth. These are the truffles that have been gathered over the last seven days, ready to be taken to the Friday morning market at Carpentras, and this week Bernard has entrusted me with an important job. I am to be the official truffle bearer, he who carries the baskets.

We set off at seven, driving almost blind through the fleece of low clouds that often settle on the hills in winter. As we dropped down on to the Carpentras road, the sun burned through, leaving wisps of cloud no more than pale smears across a sky that was as blue as July. It was going to be one of those brilliantly clear winter days when the scenery looks as though it's been polished.

The car smelled delicious, but slightly humid. I asked Bernard why it was necessary to keep the truffles damp, and he explained about the perils of evaporation. From the moment they are dug up and taken from the earth, truffles begin to dry out, losing moisture; even worse, losing weight, sometimes as much as ten percent. And since truffles are sold by weight, that ten percent is money, gone up, as Bernard said, into thin air.

By eight-thirty we were in Carpentras. So, it seemed, was every truffle enthusiast in the Vaucluse. There must have been a hundred of them, a clot of humanity on one side of the otherwise empty Place Aristide Bruant. The market takes place every Friday morning from November through March with, as you might expect, its headquarters in a bar. Those who had arrived early, now fortified by coffee and a nip of something stronger against the chill of the morning, were beginning to leave the bar to make the rounds of the trestle tables set up outside. Bernard did the same. I followed him with the baskets, attempting nonchalance, as though I was used to carrying around thousands of francs covered in damp linen.

One of the many pleasant things about the Carpentras market is that it's not confined to professionals. Anyone with a truffle to sell can try his luck with the *courtiers*—the brokers who buy for their clients in Paris or the Périgord—and I watched as one old man came sidling up to the table where a *courtier* was preparing to do business.

The old man looked from side to side before taking something wrapped in newspaper out of his pocket. He unwrapped the object, a fair-sized truffle, and presented it in cupped hands. Whether this was to conceal it from prying eyes of the competition or to enhance the aroma I wasn't sure.

"*Allez, sentez,*" said the old man. "I found it at the bottom of the garden."

The *courtier* bent over the truffle to inhale, then looked at the old man, his face a study in disbelief. "Sure," he said. "While you were taking the dog for a walk."

At that point, their negotiations were interrupted by the arrival of a gendarme, who marched through the crowd until he found a clear space in front of the tables. With a ceremonial flourish, he raised his left arm so that he could study his watch. Satisfied that the moment had officially come, he put a whistle to his mouth and blew two short blasts. "*Le marché est ouvert,*" he announced. Nine o'clock on the dot.

It was easy enough to pick out the big sellers, the *trufficulteurs*, with their bulging bags or cloth-covered baskets, and the *courtiers* at their tables. But there was no way of telling if other, anonymous buyers were making the rounds that morning. Carpentras is a well-known market, and there is always the chance that someone has come down to buy for the three-star restaurants. Consequently, if you are approached by a man expressing interest in the contents of your basket, it is not only good manners but possibly good business to offer him a sniff.

On Bernard's nod, I drew back the cloth and held up one of our baskets for a snappily dressed gentleman with a Parisian accent. His head almost disappeared inside the basket, and I could see his shoulders rise and fall as he took a series of deep breaths. He emerged smiling and nodding, then selected a truffle, which he began to scratch carefully with his thumbnail until the color and the tiny white veins below the surface showed through. As a general rule, the darker the truffle, the more perfumed and desirable it is, and therefore more expensive, because the price is linked to the smell. In other words, you're paying through the nose.

The gentleman nodded again as he replaced the truffle. He seemed highly impressed. I waited for the cash to come out. "*Merci, messieurs,*" he said, and walked off. We never saw him again. Obviously, he was nothing more than a truffle groupie, a sniffer and a scratcher rather than a buyer. Apparently, every market has one.

In fact, Bernard has regular clients that he has dealt with for years, and we would be going to see them once the buyers and sellers had stopped circling each other for long enough to establish the day's price. But for the moment, free of my responsibilities, I was able to roam and look and listen.

There is a furtive undercurrent to the truffle business. Sources of supply are kept secret. Demand is largely fuelled by cash, for which no receipts are given. Safeguards and guarantees don't exist. Irregularities—some-

times indelicately described as swindles—are not infrequent. And this year, as if to confirm the worst fears of
Monsieur Farigoule, the villainous Chinese are interfer-
ing with the French market. Their secret weapon is
the *Tuber himalayensis*, an oriental fungus that looks and
even smells like the genuine *Tuber melanosporum* from
Provence. However, there are two important differences:
The Chinese impostor sells for a fraction of the price of
a genuine truffle, and it tastes, so I am told, like rubber
shavings.

In theory there shouldn't be a problem. Side by side,
there would be no danger of confusing the varieties. But
what has happened, according to market rumor, is that
certain unscrupulous businessmen have been mixing the
two—a few genuine truffles among a batch of Chinese
fakes—and charging top prices. If there were ever to be a
popular excuse for the revival of the guillotine, this would
surely be the one.

During the first half hour or so, I had noticed that buying and selling were slow. Even so, there was a good deal
of muttering between the *courtiers* and the suppliers as
they worked toward agreeing a price per kilo. Since there
is no officially fixed price, everything is negotiable. Also, if
a seller is unhappy with the Carpentras price, there is
always the chance that a better deal might be possible at
the Saturday market farther north in Richerenches. So it
doesn't pay to rush in. It wasn't until the first big transac-
tions were made that the day's price began to settle at
around twenty-seven hundred francs per kilo.

This was the signal for portable phones to come out,
presumably so that the news could be relayed to every corner of the truffle world, and one could be sure that the
price wouldn't stay at twenty-seven hundred francs for

long. As truffles travel north, their value increases enormously, and by the time they reach Paris the price is likely to have doubled.

Business was beginning to pick up. I was standing by one of the *courtiers* scribbling a few notes when I became aware of a presence lurking close behind me and turned, almost bumping into the nose of a man peering over my shoulder to see what I was writing. I'm sure he thought I had some secret and valuable inside information. How disappointed he would have been, if he'd managed to decipher my English scrawl, to find nothing more than a few observations on what the well-dressed truffle dealers were wearing.

They wore thick-soled, dusty boots, bulky jackets with zippered inside pockets containing brown envelopes filled with cash, berets—one with an ingenious arrangement of ear flaps—modified yachting caps, a wide-brimmed black fedora, and long scarves worn bank-robber style, wrapped around to conceal the face up to eye level. It created a sinister effect, only spoiled when the scarves had to be lowered to uncover the nose for ritual sniffing.

Most of the men and women were middle-aged and of rural appearance, but there were a couple of noticeable exceptions, leather-clad young men with hard faces, cropped hair, and gold earrings. Bodyguards, I immediately thought as I looked for bulges under their jackets, probably armed and dangerous, obviously there to protect the wads of 500-franc notes that were being shuffled from hand to hand. After I had watched them for a few moments, it became clear that they were keeping their elderly mother company while she haggled over half a dozen tiny truffles in a muddy plastic bag.

Bernard decided that he was ready to sell, and we found

one of his regular contacts behind a small table at the edge
of the crowd. Like the other *courtiers,* his equipment was a
mixture of ancient and modern: a portable bar-scale of the
kind that has been in use for a good hundred years, and an
electronic pocket calculator. The truffles were examined
for color, sniffed, and transferred from the baskets to a bag
of cotton mesh. The bag was hung from the hook of the
scale, the sliding brass balance adjusted until the level of
the bar was horizontal. Bernard and the *courtier* studied it,
looked at each other, nodded. The weight was agreed. The
courtier then communed with his calculator before tapping on the keys. He showed the figures to Bernard,
screening the calculator with a hand as though he were
displaying a saucy photograph. More nodding. The price
was agreed. A check was made out (Bernard is a paragon
of legitimate practice in a murky business, and doesn't
deal in cash), and the morning's work was done.

Now for the cabaret, Bernard said, and we pushed
through the crush and into the bar. The noise was considerable, despite the secretive conversational technique that
I saw being used by many of the truffle men. They seemed
to be incapable of saying anything without shielding the
mouth with one hand each time they spoke, presumably to
foil eavesdroppers like myself. Priceless information, like
the state of their liver or the weather forecast, is therefore
kept from prying ears; or it would be, if they didn't bellow
behind the baffle of their hands.

The combination of country accents, half-swallowed
sentences, and the ever-present barrier of the hand made
conversations difficult to follow, and I managed to understand only two exchanges. The first was easier, because it
was directed at me. I'd just been introduced to one of the
dealers, a *gaillard,* a strapping hulk of a man with stomach

and voice to match his height. He asked what I thought of the market, and I told him I was impressed by the amount of money that was circulating. He nodded in agreement, his eyes flicked around the bar, and he loomed closer, one hand up against the corner of his mouth in case anyone else should overhear the force-ten whisper: "I'm rich, you know. I have five houses."

Before giving me a chance to reply, he had moved on to the end of the bar to surround a small man, wrapping one great arm around his shoulders as he leaned down, hand to mouth, ready to impart further information of a highly confidential nature. I suppose it's a habit developed over many years in a business that makes a fetish of discretion, and I wondered if it extended to his domestic life. Did he and his wife ever have a normal conversation, or was it always a succession of mutters and winks and nudges? I imagined them at the breakfast table. *"Pssst. Do you want another cup of coffee?" "Not so loud. The neighbors might hear."*

The second revelation of the morning concerned a truly remarkable item of truffling equipment; something, I think, that only a French mind could have invented. It was described with graphic gestures and a certain amount of spilled wine by a dealer who claimed to have seen it in action.

The device had been made for an old man—an extremely old man—who had been born and bred near Carpentras. For his entire adult life the truffle had been his passion. He was impatient for the coming of the first frost, and his winters were spent out on the foothills of Mont Ventoux with his dog. Each Friday he would come to the market, his linen sack crammed with a week's work. After selling his truffles, he would join the other men at the bar only long enough to have one quick drink, always a Suze, before leaving to resume the hunt. For him, a day spent away from the pursuit of truffles was a day wasted.

Time went by, and the old man's body eventually paid the price for a lifetime of stooping and crouching in bitter conditions, those years of exposure to the winds swooping down from Siberia that can make a man's kidneys ache with cold. His back gave out. It had to be kept absolutely straight. Any deviation from the perpendicular was agony, and even walking was a painful effort. His truffle hunting days were over.

Nevertheless, his passion persisted, and he was lucky enough to have a friend who brought him, each Friday, to the market. It was better than nothing, certainly, but his weekly visits turned into a source of frustration. He could look at truffles. He could scratch them. He could sniff them, but—because he couldn't bend—he could sniff only those that were placed in his hand or held under his nose. More and more, he found himself missing that thrilling headlong dive into a full basket, to be surrounded by the perfume that had been such a pleasurable part of his long life. His colleagues at the bar pondered the problem.

I was told that it was a veteran of World War II who came up with the idea, which was very loosely based on the design of the old military gas mask. It was a *museau télescopique*, or extendable snout. At one end was an abbreviated mask that covered the nose and mouth, with a wide elastic band to secure it to the head. The mask was attached to a canvas tube, pleated like the bellows of a concertina, and at the far end was the artificial nostril, an aluminum funnel. Using this ingenious extension to the nose, the old man was able to go from basket to basket, inhaling to his heart's content while keeping his back painlessly, comfortably straight. A triumph of practical medicine over cruel adversity. How I would love to have seen it in action.

By eleven o'clock the market was over. Many of the truffles that had been bought were already on trains, racing against further evaporation as they left Provence for Paris; or, in some cases, for the Dordogne, where they would be presented as natives of the Périgord. Truffles from this region are considered to be superior—like Cavaillon melons or Normandy butter—and therefore cost more. But café statistics, which I'm inclined to believe more than most, claim that up to fifty percent of the truffles sold in the Périgord originate in the Vaucluse, where prices are lower. Naturally, as with so much in the truffle business, this is unofficial. Any request for confirmation will be met by an innocent, unknowing shrug.

I know of only one fitting end to a morning spent in a truffle market, and that is a truffle lunch. You would certainly be well served at a specialist restaurant like Chez Bruno at Lorgues ("the temple of the truffle"), but Lorgues is a long way from Carpentras. Apt is closer, and in Apt you will find the Bistrot de France, a cheerful, busy restaurant on the Place de la Bouquerie. Posters on the walls, paper napkins on the tables, a convenient little bar just inside the entrance for those in urgent need, the smell of good things in the air—it's a fine, warm place to walk into after hours of standing around in the cold. All the finer because, during the season, there is always one particularly good truffle dish on the menu.

We arrived just before twelve-thirty to find the restaurant already crowded with winter customers, people from the town and nearby villages, speaking the winter language, French. (During the summer, you're more likely to hear Dutch, German, and English.) Facing the entrance were two gentlemen sitting side by side but eating alone, each at his table for one. This is a civilized arrangement that I very rarely see outside France, and I wonder why. Perhaps other nationalities feel more strongly the primitive social urge to eat in small herds. Or it may be, as Régis believes, that a Frenchman is more interested in good cooking than in bad conversation, and takes every chance he can to enjoy a solitary meal.

The tall, thin waiter with a voice like warm gravel showed us to a table, and we squeezed in next to a couple intent on the slippery joys of raw oysters on the rocks. A glance at the short, handwritten menu reassured us that the truffle supply was holding up; all we had to do was decide on the first course, and from previous visits we knew the need for caution. The chef is a believer in *cuisine copieuse*—ample and sometimes more than ample portions of everything he cooks—and it's easy to be overwhelmed before the main event.

Artichokes seemed safe enough. They arrived, half a dozen of them, *à la barigoule,* with parsley, celery, carrots, and ham in a warming, scented broth that went straight to the cockles of the heart. The people at the table next to us were by now eating their main course, a beef stew, using their forks to cut the meat and using pieces of bread, like edible cutlery, to guide each mouthful onto the fork. Bad manners in polite society, no doubt, but very practical if you want to eat a *daube* without sacrificing the juice.

One of the less obvious signs of a well-run, professional restaurant is the sense of timing displayed by the waiters, the rhythm of lunch. If the service is too slow, there is a tendency to eat too much bread and drink too much wine. This is bad, but the opposite is worse. If the service is too quick, if the waiter hovers and bustles and tries to steal my plate before I've wiped off the gravy, if I can feel his breath on the back of my neck and his fingers drumming on the back of my chair while I'm choosing a cheese, it ruins everything. My palate barely has time to take in one taste before having to adjust to the next. I feel jostled and unwanted. Lunch has been turned into a speed trial.

Pauses are essential; a few minutes between courses to allow the appetite to recover and anticipation to set in, a chance to enjoy the moment, to look around and to eaves-drop. I have a terrible weakness for collecting snatches of other people's conversations, and occasionally I'm rewarded with unusual fragments of knowledge. My fa-vorite of the day came from a large but shapely woman sit-ting nearby whom I learned was the owner of a local lingerie shop. "*Beh oui,*" she said to her companion, wav-ing her spoon for emphasis, "*il faut du temps pour la corsetterie.*" You can't argue with that. I made a mental note not to rush things next time I was shopping for a corset, and leaned back to allow the waiter through with the main course.

It was a *brouillade de truffes*—the classic combination of lightly scrambled eggs studded with slices of black truf-fle, served in a high-sided copper saucepan that was left between us on the table. We were two. There was easily enough *brouillade* for three, presumably to allow for any evaporation that might have taken place on the journey from the kitchen. Fork in one hand, bread in the other, a grateful nod in the direction of St. Antoine, the patron saint of truffle growers, and we started to eat.

The flavor of a truffle is the continuation of its scent, complex and earthy, neither mushroom nor meat, but something in between. It tastes, more than anything else I know, of the outdoors, and there is a nicely balanced contrast in the mouth between the crunchy texture of the truffle and the bland smoothness of the eggs. You will find truffles in dozens of more elaborate recipes, from a millionaire's ravioli to a Sunday-best chicken, but I don't think you can beat simplicity. Eggs, scrambled or in an omelet, make the perfect background.

We somehow finished the third person's portion between us, and rested. The local corset expert was talking about the benefits to one's *forme* of correct posture. The thrust of her argument, delivered between mouthfuls of apple crumble and cream, was that you could eat what you wanted as long as you sat up straight and wore sufficiently sturdy and supportive undergarments. I wondered if the editors of *Vogue* were aware of this.

The tempo of the restaurant had slowed. Appetites had been satisfied, although the more ambitious customers were still showing signs of life over the choice of desserts. I felt I should have a taste of cheese, a bite, just a little something to go with the last glass of wine. Modest servings, however, were not on the menu. An entire Banon arrived, a puck of cheese wrapped in dried chestnut leaves and tied with raffia, firm on the outside, softening by degrees to an almost liquid center, salty, creamy, and pungent. Somehow that, too, disappeared.

A wonderful, simple lunch. Nothing to it, really, apart from excellent ingredients and a chef with the confidence and good sense not to muffle their flavors with unnecessary sauces and trimmings. Leave well enough alone, serve plenty of it, and respect the seasons is his formula. When truffles are fresh, serve truffles; when strawberries are at their best, serve strawberries. I suppose this might be considered a slightly old-fashioned way to run a restaurant. After all, in these modern times everything from asparagus to venison comes to the table by plane and is available all through the year. Heaven knows where it all originates—hothouses, food factories, or different hemispheres, I imagine—but there it is, whatever you want, at a price. Or rather, several prices.

It costs more, obviously. It won't be as fresh as local food, despite the miracles of refrigerated travel and a process that I've heard described as ripeness retardation. And, worst of all, it ignores the calendar, so there is none of the anticipation, none of the pleasure to be had from the year's first glorious dish of a seasonal delicacy. It's a great shame to miss that.

Spring is coming. Soon the *courtiers* of Carpentras will put away their scales and their adding machines, the gendarme will be able to give his whistle a rest, and the market will close down. The poachers and their dogs will move on, doubtless to some other nefarious activity. The chef at the Bistrot de France will change his menu, and fresh truffles won't be seen again until the end of the year. But I'm happy to wait. Even for truffles, I'm happy to wait.

Green Thumbs
and Black Tomatoes

It must be at least twenty years ago that garden chic began to spread, like a delicate high-priced creeper, across the plains and valleys of the Luberon.

It came in the wake of the refugees who made their escape every year from the dank climates of the north. There was no doubt that they loved their second homes in Provence. They loved the light and the dry heat. And yet, looking around them once the novelty of sustained, predictable sunshine had worn off, they found that there was something missing. The countryside—mostly the grays and greens of weathered limestone crags and wizened scrub oaks—was striking and often spectacular. But it was also—well, a little *bare*.

There was lavender, broom, and rosemary, of course, and vines and cherry trees, maybe even a dusty, long-suffering almond or two. But these weren't enough to cure the itch for something more lush. The refugees began to pine for conspicuous color and ornamental vegetation. They missed their shady bowers and their flowerbeds. They wanted what they would call a proper garden—a riot of roses, great swags of wisteria to soften all that stone, trees that were noticeably taller than they were. And so, with a brave disregard for local conditions, they set about planning decorative oases among the rocky fields and terraced hillsides.

The climate, the soil, and the lack of water were major problems; human nature, unwilling to wait for results, was another. Gardens created from scratch can take anything from ten to twenty-five years before they reach the desirable, photogenic state of luxuriant maturity. Plane trees, oaks, and olives need much longer. The classic recipe for a lawn—seed, then mow and roll for two hundred years—puts an even greater strain on a garden-lover's patience. It was clear that nature was sadly lacking in vim and acceleration, and couldn't possibly be left to her own devices. Who wants to spend a lifetime of summers surrounded by twigs?

The impatience of foreigners was, at first, a source of local bewilderment. What was the hurry, why the rush? In an agricultural society, accustomed to the slow turn of seasons and an annual growth rate measured in millimeters, the idea of tinkering with the pace of nature was unknown. But it didn't take too long for the penny to drop, and the refugees' urge for rapid results eventually turned into a blessing. In fact, it has spawned an industry: instant gardens, shipped in and set up with astonishing speed, astonishing skill, and, it must be said, at astonishing cost.

More often than not, the process begins below ground level. Before anything can be planted, there is the question of what it should be planted in, and immediately we come up against the difference between fertile earth and plain old land. The first exploratory digs in the garden-to-be are not encouraging. Thin, parched stuff it is, more stone than anything else, sprinkled with reminders of the previous owner: fragments of crockery, rusty oil cans, twisted bicycle wheels, pastis bottles, the odd decomposing boot. That won't do at all. What you need, Monsieur, for the garden of your dreams, are tons—many tons—of good rich soil. And of course, since water is the lifeblood of a garden, an irrigation system to keep it from drying out. Only then can we commence with the business of planting.

All at once, there are intimations of bankruptcy, and for some people this is the moment when they rediscover the simple charms of thyme and lavender, which manage to exist and even thrive without imported soil or imported water. But other, braver souls, more visionary, more determined, or just richer, take a deep breath, dig into their pockets, and carry on.

Bulldozers to level the land arrive first, leaving behind giant banks of rocks and roots and any bushes unfortunate enough to have been standing in the path of progress. These unsightly humps have to be taken away. The removal squad is then followed by convoys of trucks—trucks piled high with earth excavated from some distant, more fertile spot, trucks packed tight with roses, oleanders, and sacks of fertilizer, trucks with lawns rolled up like carpets, trucks with ready-made topiary gardens of box and holly, beautifully barbered into cones and spheres. And then there are the cornerstones of garden architecture, the trees.

It is not uncommon to see mobile forests swaying along the roads before they disappear up secluded driveways: plane trees to make a long, sweeping *allée* up to the house, olive trees to guard the pool, lindens, cypresses, and chestnuts to charm the eye on a summer's evening. They are all well past their adolescence and into early maturity, their root balls encased in giant tubs or bound in burlap. It's an impressive sight. It will be an impressive garden—and a truly spectacular bill.

Over the years, *pépiniéristes*, or nursery gardeners, have sprung up throughout Provence like the buds of spring. They are even more numerous than real estate agents; hundreds of them take up eleven closely spaced columns in the Yellow Pages of the Vaucluse telephone directory. Their premises vary in size from a hut on the edge of a small field to more elaborate establishments set among several acres smothered in growth, and it was to one of these that I went in search of inspiration and a pot of geraniums.

The garden empire of Monsieur Appy is situated below Roussillon, a village with the flushed complexion of a face that has taken too much sun; a baked, ruddy village, built with stone from the nearby ochre quarries. As you drive down the hill and take the road to Gordes, the red-tinged earth fades into brown and the vines march across the fields in orderly, immaculate ranks as the land flattens out. And then, in the distance, the curved shape of a transparent roof can be seen above a row of treetops.

To describe it as a greenhouse doesn't do it justice. It's

the size of a hangar. A baby Boeing could be put in there to ripen and sprout wings in the warmth, and there would still be room for a modest jungle in the back. On one hot afternoon when I was there, it even smelt like a jungle; the atmosphere was close and humid, the whiff of fertility hung in the air, and it wouldn't have surprised me to see a monkey—no doubt gibbering in a Provençal accent—peering at me from behind a cluster of azalea bushes.

It's rare to see so much concentrated green, or so many shades of green, every leaf shining with health—yuccas, gardenias, ficus trees with slender plaited trunks, annuals and perennials, improbably perfect shrubs. I felt sure that on a quiet day you could actually hear the sound of them growing—a moist whisper—but the days are seldom that quiet. Men are constantly on the move between the long rows with barrows and trays of plants. Garden designers with their clients refer to landscape plans and make notes, occasionally running their fingers through the hair of a particularly well endowed fern. Trucks and cars come and go by the entrance, loading up with the contents of future flowerbeds and ornamental shrubberies. It's a remarkable enterprise, the furthest thing one could imagine from nature in the raw, an enormous display of disciplined cultivation; and that's just the main greenhouse.

Larger and more hardy specimens are kept on the other side of the road. This is the forest department, where you will find hundred-year-old olive trees and twenty-foot cypresses, rows of them, next to just about every other kind of tree that can survive in Provence. To one side is the topiary headquarters, filled with box clipped into *boules,* pyramids, and rather stout, long-necked birds. I saw one extraordinary bush that had been fashioned into the form of a snake. It must have been a good five feet tall, and, according to my amateur calculations, at least sixty years old. My experience with box is that it grows little more than an inch a year. But then, I don't have the green thumb of Monsieur Appy.

He's usually there, genial and immensely knowledge-able, darting among his plants and clients, dispensing advice on everything from bone meal to slug control, help-ing to load your car while giving you a five-minute course on pruning. There's a noticeable twinkle to his eye, and judging by the size of his business he has much to twinkle about. He deserves his success. I can't think of a better place to go if you want to turn an unpromising patch of scrub into a small green masterpiece; or even a large green masterpiece, a modern Versailles.

I have mixed feelings about gardens on the grand scale. I can't help admiring the effort, the optimism, the invest-ment, the skill of the *pépiniériste* and the end results, which are often superb. I've seen some of them, and you would swear they had been established in the nineteenth century rather than a few years ago. But would I want a garden like that, with its constant need to be nourished by a mulch of 500-franc notes? I don't think so. It would be a full-time job and an endless responsibility trying to keep nature under control, and I know that nature would win; she has more stamina than I do, and never stops for lunch.

Some time ago I decided that Versailles was not for me. I would be happy to settle for something less grandiose and more manageable, and I've been lucky enough to find just the man to help me.

Jean-Luc Danneyrolles specializes in the edible garden, the *potager*. Other gardening experts and landscape artists will have you swooning at their descriptions of vistas and arbors, leafy walkways and pleached limes; Jean-Luc can go into raptures over a carrot.

I first heard about him from a friend. The two of them were taking a winter walk when Jean-Luc suddenly stopped as he came to a seemingly ordinary oak, wind-blown and stunted like hundreds of others. But he had noticed a roughly circular, burnt-looking area of earth around the base of the tree. Dropping down on all fours, he sniffed the earth, scratched at the surface, sniffed again. Then he dug down with his hands, very gently, and came up with a truffle.

Having heard the story, I couldn't wait to meet him. I imagined a mythic creature, half man, half hound, a human version of one of Bernard's truffle dogs, low-slung and hirsute, possibly with a large wet nose. When we finally did meet, the reality was considerably more hand-some: thick black hair, penetrating brown eyes, and a smile that would do credit to a Hollywood dentist. He was reassuringly human. And yet, as I came to know him, I noticed something about Jean-Luc that set him apart from other men, even other men who collaborate with nature to make their living. He has a quite uncanny affinity with the earth; almost as if he can see through it. He is able, for instance, to walk across a piece of land that hundreds have walked across before and find something nobody else has found.

We were in his office one day—a gardener's office with boots in the corner, packets of seeds in the filing drawers, and the clean, sharp scent of burning eucalyptus coming from an iron stove—when he asked if I would like to see what he called his icons. They were chippings from his-tory, all of them discovered by Jean-Luc in the fields around his house. It's an area that he describes as a *poubelle antique,* or an ancient rubbish dump, a repository of bits and pieces lost or discarded in the course of six thousand years or so of human habitation.

He picked out a selection of miniature ax-heads, some no bigger than a book of matches. They were stones gathered long ago from the bed of the Durance River, then shaped, sharpened, and polished until they had the dull gleam of oiled slate. They looked like infant tomahawks, obviously too small to have been used as weapons. In fact, they were tools made by Neolithic man, "the inventor of agriculture," and used as we would use a mechanical brush-cutter today to clear tangles of light undergrowth. Gardening must have been a quieter business altogether in the Stone Age.

Jean-Luc laid more discoveries out on the table, and we changed civilizations. There were Roman coins, slightly frayed at the edges by the wear of centuries, but still bearing recognizable images. On one, the blurred profile was identified by a few legible letters as Augustus Caesar; on another, the form of a woman seated beside an amphora. There was part of a life-sized marble finger from a statue. There was a perfectly cut cube of deep-blue mosaic. And there were dozens of terra-cotta fragments, some inscribed with the names of their Roman makers, some merely marked with a broad straight groove left by a Roman thumb.

"What do you make of that?" Jean-Luc grinned as he pushed an almost flat, almost square piece of pottery across the table. It was smaller than the palm of my hand, a tiny but clearly detailed study of a naked couple—shown from the head down, presumably for the sake of their reputations—caught enjoying a moment of sexual acrobatics, a Roman dirty joke. Was it part of a dish, brought out on appropriate occasions? And what would those be? Orgies? Weddings? Bar Mitzvahs? Or was it just typical of the style of the age, the kind of everyday decorative refinement that any genteel middle-class Roman family would be happy to put on the table when the neighbors came round for dinner?

It felt strange to hold this in my hand and look through the window at the modern world: telephone poles, a parked car, a tarmac road. Man had been living here, exactly where we were sitting, for thousands of years, leaving behind relics of the kind that we put in museums: art and artifacts, often fascinating and sometimes beautiful. I couldn't imagine that the leavings of the twentieth century—the blobs of plastic and metal and the assortment of nuclear souvenirs—would hold the same interest.

I asked Jean-Luc how he could explain his success in finding what other people had overlooked. *"C'est le regard du jardinier,"* he said. The gardener's eye, which studies the earth instead of just looking at it. I know it's not as simple as that, but he insists that it is. For him, part-time archaeology is no more than a hobby.

Work is vegetables. Most Saturday mornings, he is at his stand in the Apt market, where he sells his produce. All of it is raised *à la façon biologique*—that is, without the dubious benefits of chemicals: no pesticides, no weed-killers, no cocktails of growth stimulants, no tweaking of nature. When I told Jean-Luc I had seen a shop in California—I think it was called a vegetable boutique—selling tomatoes that were square, for easier storage in the refrigerator, he was silent. His expression said everything that was necessary.

He has been growing his own vegetables naturally for

years, long before nature became fashionable. Enthusiastic articles about the return to the earth tend to irritate him. Serious gardeners, he says, never left the earth. But the revival of interest in organically grown food has made him something of a vegetable guru in France. He is the author of an elegant little book about onions and garlic—the first food book I've seen that includes tips on how to repel vampire bats—and has just finished another on tomatoes. Now he finds himself being called in to create *potagers* for others. He will design your kitchen garden, stock it, and tell you how to make it flourish. If you ask him nicely, he might even come and eat some of it with you.

His most celebrated client is Alain Ducasse, currently the most decorated chef in France with six Michelin stars. Ducasse has a restaurant in Paris (three stars), another in Monte Carlo (three stars), and more recently a third in Haute Provence, at Moustiers Sainte Marie. It was here in Moustiers that Jean-Luc planned and planted a *potager* fit for a prince of gastronomy; not just a routine affair with rows of conventional peas, beans, and lettuces, but a modern home for some ancient and almost forgotten vegetables.

These he collects from all over the country. He has sometimes come across them growing wild in the fields, or struggling to survive among the weeds of someone else's long-abandoned kitchen garden. He has contacts among other gardeners, much older than himself, who give him seeds that are descended from seeds given to them by even older gardeners. He studies the classic books, like Vilmorin's *Les Plantes Potagères*, published in 1890, which describes the vegetables our ancestors used to eat. In this way, he has rediscovered a distant, tender cousin of the parsnip, a whole range of aromatic herbs, and an oddity that I think might have a great future.

It has the instantly familiar form and surface texture of a tomato, but it's a black tomato. Or, depending on the light in which you see it, a deep-purple tomato, not unlike the color of an eggplant. The taste is delicate, perhaps slightly stronger than a red tomato, and the visual effect is dusky and dramatic. I can see it becoming wildly popular with chefs who have a weakness for large white plates and picturesque salads. With luck, it might even put the square tomato out of business.

The last time I saw Jean-Luc, he was working on an exhibit for a gardening festival to be held in Chaumont. He had planned the perfect *potager,* and before starting the real thing he had laid out a scale model on a sheet of plywood, a miniature education in garden design.

There would be a hundred and fifty varieties of plants arranged in four squares: herbs, flowering vegetables, fruiting vegetables, and root vegetables, each square contained within its own tight little border of low box bushes. The gravel paths dividing the squares made the form of a cross. In the center, where the paths met, there would be a tree that Jean-Luc had found, the skeleton of an old olive that had frozen to death in the winter of 1956. And at the far end was the *gloriette,* a dignified version of the garden shed with a steep, pointed roof.

The various elements were shown on the main model by even smaller models. Different colors of tissue paper, in rows of microscopic tufts, indicated the different vegetables: a layer of gravel specks for the paths, a spreading twig for the tree, everything to scale in a garden that was a testament to the Gallic passion for neatness, order, and symmetry. Let a Frenchman loose in the great outdoors, and the first thing he'll want to do is organize it; then he will see if there are ways of eating it. The kitchen garden satisfies both requirements, a thing of beauty and a joy for dinner.

I have to admit I would love a garden like that, and I asked Jean-Luc if he would consider designing one for us—something modest, nothing more than a large handkerchief of land which we could turn into a home for black tomatoes and tender turnips.

He said he'd be happy to think about it when he came back from New York. He and his wife were spending a week there; it would be their first time in America, and they had no idea what to expect. I had bought him a map of Manhattan, and while he looked at it I tried to think of parts of the city he might find particularly interesting.

But where do you send a professional gardener on his first visit to New York? Central Park seemed like an obvious suggestion, and certainly its size—almost twice as big as the entire principality of Monaco—would impress Jean-Luc. But I wondered if his gardener's soul would be offended by the sprawl of it, the winding, random nature of its paths, the absence of straight lines, the undisciplined trees, the general lack of formality. And he'd have to be warned about the health hazards lurking in the park, from lethally indigestible hot dogs to muggers on Rollerblades.

But I thought he would like the way nature was contained along Park Avenue, with its spring plantings of flowers and, just visible high above the traffic, the aerial groves of millionaires' roof gardens.

As for vegetables, he would find that they were larger, glossier, and more numerous than he was used to. Nothing would be out of season. And he would have his first exposure to the Korean greengrocers who seem to have taken over the vegetable business in Manhattan. Unfortunately, comparing notes with fellow professionals would be tricky, although I liked the thought of a Korean and a Provençal trying to discuss the fine points of zucchini without the benefit of a common language.

In the end, I decided on just one suggestion. If Jean-Luc wanted to see some green—some serious green—being cultivated, the Stock Exchange was the place to go.

He looked up from the map, shaking his head in astonishment, enchanted by the symmetrical grid of midtown Manhattan.

"I never realized it was so logical," he said, "so easy."

"It's fun, too," I said. "Great fun. But you'll find the speed of it a bit of a shock after Provence. Everybody's in a hurry."

"Why?"

There are times when a shrug is the only answer.

P.S.

Eleven years ago, more by accident than design, I wrote *A Year in Provence*. It would be surprising if changes hadn't taken place during the time that has passed, and it has been said, particularly by the British press, that I have contributed to some of those changes. One of my crimes is to have encouraged people to visit the region. Too many people—*far* too many people—if the reports were to be believed. Worse still, they were people of the wrong sort. One marvelously eccentric newspaper article claimed that my book had inspired busloads of English football hooligans (not a group noted for its voracious reading habits) to descend on the Luberon. We were assured that they would be awash with beer and bristling with violent intentions. Horrors of pillage, debauchery, and destruction were hinted at with great glee. But since nobody had bothered to inform the hooligans, they didn't come. The story died.

It was replaced by other invasion stories, most of them written from vantage points a thousand miles away on the other side of the Channel, lamenting the end of Provence as an unspoiled area. It was interesting to compare what the articles said with what I saw when I looked out of the window: More often than not, the view would be of a deserted road and a deserted valley. Very little in the way of hordes.

Now, eleven years later, not much has changed. The neighborhood wines have improved enormously, and there is a greater choice of restaurants. Some of the more popular villages, such as Gordes and Bonnieux, become crowded in July and August. But the unattractive monuments to mass tourism—those three-hundred-room hotels and theme parks and condominium colonies—don't exist, and never will as long as current building restrictions remain in force. Provence is still beautiful. Vast areas of it are still wild and empty. Peace and silence, which have become endangered commodities in the modern world, are still available. The old men still play their endless games of *boules*. The markets are as colorful and abundant as ever. There is room to breathe, and the air is clean.

More than anything else, people make a place, and the local inhabitants don't seem to have changed at all. I'm happy to have this chance to thank them for the warmth of their welcome and their many kindnesses. We were made to feel that we had come home.